The Encapsulated Man

An Interdisciplinary Essay
on the Search for Meaning

by

JOSEPH R. ROYCE
University of Alberta

AN INSIGHT BOOK

D. VAN NOSTRAND COMPANY, INC.

PRINCETON, NEW JERSEY

TORONTO   LONDON

NEW YORK

DEDICATED TO THE CREATIVE MINORITY,
MOST OF WHOM ARE ENCAPSULATED
BUT AT LEAST AWARE

D. VAN NOSTRAND COMPANY, INC.
120 Alexander St., Princeton, New Jersey
(*Principal Office*)
24 West 40 Street, New York 18, New York

D. VAN NOSTRAND COMPANY, LTD.
358, Kensington High Street, London, W.14, England

D. VAN NOSTRAND COMPANY (Canada), LTD.
25 Hollinger Road, Toronto 16, Canada

PRINTED IN THE UNITED STATES OF AMERICA

Preface

I have been among a variety of knowledge specialists inside and outside academic halls as student, professor, management and personnel consultant, aviation psychologist, and researcher since 1937. During the course of these twenty-five years I have been led down many narrow pathways, both within my area of special study and outside it. At various times I have been told that "real truth" lies in this direction, that direction, or along another direction. I have heard humanities professors claim that scientists are uneducated, I have heard experimentally oriented scientists suggest that theoreticians ought not to be permitted on the premises, and I have heard theoretical scientists denounce the pebble-picking efforts of experimentalists. I have worked with biologists who would not discuss anything unless it could somehow be seen, touched, smelled, or otherwise sensed. I have heard mathematicians point out how they were working toward truth at its highest level, and that the sensory level of the experimental scientist is so pedestrian as to be at best a questionable endeavor for really big minds. And finally, I have known artists and literary men who regard scientists as a mob of savages. In short, I have repeatedly been led to believe by my faculty colleagues and other specialists that I could really get the answers to things if I would simply follow them down the righteous path of their particular discipline. I am, of course, talking about an attitude which goes beyond mere enthusiasm and concern for one's subject. I am talking about the very strong beliefs of "specialists" and the rather narrow view which this kind of experience can cultivate. Of course, this provincialism is not confined to academic specialists. It is equally, or perhaps even more, evident among specialists everywhere, in management, labor, and the professions.

In the year 1955 it was my good fortune to be invited to participate as a Faculty Fellow in a Ford Foundation-sponsored experiment in interdisciplinary education. This program, The Inter-collegiate Program of Graduate Studies in the Humanities and Social Sciences, is conducted cooperatively by seven liberal arts colleges in southern California: Claremont Graduate School, Claremont Men's College, Occidental College, Pomona College, University of Redlands, Scripps College, and Whittier College. Very briefly, this doctoral-level program is concerned with developing breadth of education along with the usual depth. A major feature of this program is the intersubject seminar. An interdisciplinary seminar might include four or five professors from as many different disciplines, plus from ten to twenty students representing a wide variety of fields of study. The diverse members of the seminar come to grips with a general area of inquiry from their special perspectives. For example, in 1955-1956 I participated in a seminar called "The Nature of Institutions." I was joined in this common search by an economist, a sociologist, a political scientist, and an historian. I served as coordinator of two similar seminars on "Science and Civilization" and "The Nature of Man," non-Ford Foundation experimental efforts for seniors and graduate students at the University of Redlands, during the years 1956-1957 and 1958-1960, and a graduate seminar on philosophy and psychology at the University of Alberta in 1961-1962. The Science and Civilization seminar involved the combined thinking of a psychologist, a physicist, a chemist, and a sociologist. The seminar on man involved a chemist, a sociologist-anthropologist, a political scientist, and a psychologist; and the psychology-philosophy seminar involved a philosopher, a psychologist, and a biologist. During the year 1957-1958 I participated in another inter-collegiate interdisciplinary seminar on Standards of Judgment, involving a philosopher, an economist, a professor of literature, and myself as a representative of psychology.

While I had been slowly developing beyond my particular specialty within theoretical-experimental psychology, namely, the factorial analysis of animal behavior, toward becoming a "general specialist," a psychologist, it was my experience in the multidisciplinary seminars mentioned above that was primarily responsible for my personal efforts to become an unencapsulated man. This book represents one encapsulated man's views as to why "specialization" is a profoundly serious problem in today's world, why we must remove some cobwebs in our thinking on this matter and at least seriously entertain the idea of developing "generalists" as well as "specialists." It is an attempt to focus on a world view as a generalist rather than as a specialist, in terms of the problem rather than from the point of view of a discipline. It is, therefore, a multidisciplinary effort to view the nature of reality as a totality rather than piecemeal. In short, I attempt to draw on whatever knowledge is relevant to the problem although I am obviously limited by my special exposure to the field of psychology. In the process special consideration is given to problems of epistemology, the 20th-century malady of meaninglessness, existentialism, logical positivism, the psychology of cognition, perception, meaning, value, and personality, and the reality significance of the symbol and the myth.

I am fully aware of the magnitude, and in a real sense of the impossibility, of the task I have set for myself. While I feel my personal inadequacy for dealing with this problem most keenly, I offer no apology for having made the attempt, and I invite your criticism and comments as aids in continuing the search.

JOSEPH R. ROYCE

Edmonton, Alberta
Canada

ACKNOWLEDGMENTS

This book grew out of my participation in a Ford Foundation experimental program in multi-disciplinary graduate education. I am, therefore, grateful to the Ford Foundation for providing the funds which released me during the academic years 1955-1956 and 1957-1958 from a portion of my teaching duties at the University of Redlands so that I might participate part-time as a Faculty Fellow in the Inter-collegiate Program of Graduate Studies. I am also grateful to the University of Redlands for reducing my teaching load during the years 1956-1957 and 1958-1960 so that I could coordinate similar multidisciplinary seminars held on the Redlands campus under University sponsorship. This effort would not have gotten off the ground, however, had I not been granted a sabbatical leave of absence from the University of Redlands, which I elected to take during three consecutive summers between 1958 and 1960.

Various portions of the book were improved by feedback as a result of presentations to seminars, conferences, and classroom lectures. In this connection I am thinking particularly of the conferences on science and religion on the east coast (Institute on Religion in an Age of Science) and the west coast (Conference on Science and Religion), the "working group" on psychology and religion (David Bakan, W. H. Clark, C. A. Curran, J. Dittes, Joseph Havens, K. W. Irwin, Robert C. Kimball, Robert B. MacLeod, Paul W. Pruyser, and myself), and the interdisciplinary seminars in the Ford program (Inter-collegiate Program of Graduate Studies) and at the University of Redlands. I must similarly acknowledge such feedback from both students and staff at the University of Alberta with whom I have participated in the interdepartmental seminar in philosophy and psychology.

Certain individuals have been a source of great help and stimulation in the completion of this effort, in particular, my friend and faculty colleague in literature at the University of Redlands, Mr. Jack Lewis. Much of what is written here is a result of a more or less continuous dialogue with Mr. Lewis on the issues of this book during the years 1956-1960. In addition, he has offered faithful and serious critical review of the total final output. Similar acknowledgments for critical review of portions of the manuscript are extended to my University of Alberta colleagues Ludwig von Bertalanffy (biology and psychology) and Charles Hobart (sociology) and to colleagues at other locations, including Donald T. Campbell (psychology), Joseph Havens (psychology and religion), Milton Hunnex (philosophy), Robert Kimball (theology), and F. A. Kingsbury (psychology). While the critical reviewers mentioned above have saved me from going astray on particular points, sole responsibility for remaining errors must be mine.

The writer also wishes to acknowledge the general assistance he has received from a departmental colleague, Professor Lolita Wilson, and from two able departmental secretaries, Joan Frederick and Margaret Myers.

Finally, there is the incalculable aid and assistance which has come to me from my wife, for she has been a true partner in this venture, having provided me both with original leads and with critical reaction on many sections of the manuscript.

I have published the following papers in the period 1957-1962 on the subject of this book. Those portions of the cited papers which relate to the book are given in parentheses.

Toward the Advancement of Theoretical Psychology, *Psychological Reports*, 1957, 3, 401-410 (55-58).

Factor Theory and Genetics, *Educational and Psychological Measurement*, 1957, 17, 361-376 (86-87).

The Search for Meaning, *American Scientist*, 1959, 47, 515-535; first presented as an invited address to the Institute on Religion in an Age of Science, August, 1958, Fifth Annual Summer Conference, Star Island, New Hampshire (a brief version of the entire book).

The Problem of Meaninglessness, *Proceedings of the Conference on Science and Religion*, 1959, 2, 9-13; presented at the second annual conference at the California Institute of Technology, Pasadena, California (69-72).

The Problem of Encapsulation, *Journal of Existential Psychiatry*, 1961, 1, 426-440 (30-44).

Educating the Generalist, *Main Currents in Modern Thought*, 1961, 17, 99-103 (183-194).

Psychology, Existentialism, and Religion, *Journal of General Psychology*, 1962, 66, 3-16 presented in a Symposium on Existentialism and Psychotherapy at the 1958 annual meeting of the Western Psychological Association, San Diego, California and as an invited address to the Institute on Religion in an Age of Science, August, 1961,

Eighth Annual Summer Conference, Star Island, New Hampshire (112-122).

On Two Cultures and Contemporary Psychology (a comment), *American Psychologist*, 1962, 17, 260 (28-29).

Psychology at the Crossroads Between the Sciences and the Humanities. In J. R. Royce (editor), *Interdisciplinary Analysis of the Symbol: Implications for Psychology*, New York: Random House, in press (47-55).

Contents

"*The whole visible world is only an imperceptible atom in the ample bosom of nature. No idea approaches it. We may enlarge our conceptions beyond all imaginable space; we can only produce atoms in comparison with the reality of things. It is an infinite sphere, the center of which is everywhere, the circumference nowhere.*"

—BLAISE PASCAL

"*. . . let any man open his eyes to the world he lives in, and he'll become an Outsider immediately. He will begin by thinking he sees 'too deep and too much'; he will end by realizing that you cannot see too deep and too much.*"

—GEORGE FOX

"*A planned life is closed; it can be endured, but it cannot be lived.*"

—ALAN BURGESS

"*. . . much of the evil in the world is due to the fact that man in general is hopelessly unconscious. . . .*"

—C. G. JUNG

"*. . . we must make the necessary effort . . . to break our way out of the prison walls of the local and shortlived histories of our own countries and our own cultures, and we must accustom ourselves to taking a synoptic view of history as a whole.*"

—ARNOLD TOYNBEE

1

Introduction and Overview

"The isolated knowledge obtained by a group of specialists in a narrow field has in itself no value whatsoever, but only in its synthesis with all the rest of knowledge and only inasmuch as it really contributes in this synthesis something toward answering the demand, 'Who are we?'"

—ERWIN SCHRÖDINGER

One of the qualities which marks man as distinctively human is his insistent quest for the meaning of things. The question is one that faces "everyman" from the child's first awareness of the mystery of life to the adult's apprehension of the mystery of death. As one existential writer put it, "I know only two things—one, that I will be dead someday; two, that I am not dead now. The only question is what shall I do between those two points." Does nihilistic literature and philosophy have the answer—wallowing in nothingness? Are the Madison Avenue thought controllers right in their claim that the time for the individual has passed and that we should conform to collectivities because there is safety in numbers? Shall we follow the "beat generation" and the "angry young men" who say we should conform to non-conformity in the name of pure rebelliousness and non-constructive creativity? Or should we just capitulate with the "positive thinkers" who say that all this concern about what things mean is too nerve wracking and that the problems of life can best be met by taking existential tranquilizers in the form of sugar-coated mottoes?

The way in which modern man is clutching at straws in his search for meaning is symptomatic both of the depth of his concern and of the inadequacy of the answers which are emerging. Material advances, while not necessarily contrary to the public good, do not guarantee what the American rather naïvely and immodestly calls "progress." Middle and Far Eastern countries do not

1

necessarily leap at the opportunity to adopt the American
Way when it is offered to them by an eager Uncle Sam.
And advanced technology can no longer guarantee a
favorable international balance of power because of the
threat of total extinction. The sunny optimism of a fron-
tier-oriented America is currently being challenged by the
unbounded zeal of rising Communism. The formerly subjugated people of Africa and Asia are awakening to the
possibilities of self-determination and are properly demanding national independence. And 20th-century history clearly demonstrates that the so-called rational West
has been the source of the greatest devastation and irrationality known to civilized man. Contemporary man,
especially Western man, is confused by all this, and he
is searching for a new sense of orientation to life. Contemporary man finds himself in a paradoxical predicament. He has more political freedom, more personal
freedom from the slavery of hard work, and better health
and more material advantages than his predecessors.
While, in general, man has never had it so good, the
future of mankind has never looked so bad. For the contemporary paradox of the human predicament is that in
spite of possessing all the earmarks of happiness, the
inner man has rarely been more miserable. The situation
can be summed up by saying that contemporary man is
suffering from the malady of meaninglessness. Modern
movements such as existentialism and the revival of interest in religion point rather decisively to the inadequacy
of traditional values. And the restless searching which is
manifest in the major cultural outlets, such as the arts and
science, are indicative of the inability of traditional symbols to carry the weight of a meaningful existence. This
book concerns itself with this search for meaning, particularly the search of 20th-century man.

My thesis is that such a search demands total involvement and maximum awareness, but that man is encapsulated. By encapsulated I mean claiming to have the
whole of truth when one has only part of it. By encapsulated I mean looking at life partially and proceeding to
make statements concerning the whole of life. And by
encapsulated I mean living partially because one's daily
activities are based on a world-view or philosophy of life

which is meager next to the larger meaning of existence. Thus, this book focuses its attention on the dilemma of contemporary specialism, that is, specialism in living as well as specialism in work. I mean, in other words, the outlook that only certain views are correct and that only certain people have the proper background to have these views. I mean the narrowing down of vocational tasks brought on by the industrial revolution and resulting in twenty different "experts" making a shoe rather than one master shoemaker. I mean the situation in which a person dares not comment "outside his field" and feels that he must take a course in electrical engineering before replacing a light bulb. I mean those policies which are promulgated as supra-national but are, in fact, nationalistic in intent. I mean, in short, the fragmentary ethos of the 20th century. A major concern is the emaciated texture of the specialist's day-to-day living. This concern plunges us into the existential center of man and requires that we explore deeply such problems as value and personality. Another major concern is the narrowness of the specialist in his search for truth. The dilemma of the specialist as truth-seeker is that he has not seen much of the universe from the black bottom of his nicely furrowed rut, but he proceeds to proclaim his world view anyhow and, in many cases with considerable vigor. This concern takes us into the problem of epistemological relativism, value relativism, and the consequent feeling of despair and meaninglessness. Thus the dilemma of specialism is partialness or meaninglessness, on both an existential or daily-living level and at the level of coming to grips with reality or truth.

The inquiry opens with the question of knowledge and reality. In Chapter 2 I describe four basic ways of knowing: rationalism, intuitionism, empiricism, and authoritarianism. Each of these involves a different criterion for establishing truth and therefore a different reality continuum. Thus, each of these approaches, while epistemologically valid, is limited to a particular way of looking at things. This point is elaborated in an analysis of the epistemological basis of the various special disciplines of knowledge, especially those of science and religion.

The legitimacy of different approaches to reality points

up the problem of encapsulation, for in Chapter 2 we note the tendency for each of the major epistemologies to claim priority in dealing with "the truth." In Chapter 3 I explore basic concepts and definitions, including three different levels of encapsulated man: the man who claims a view of ultimate reality, the man who claims a world-view, and the man who sees the world in such terms as America first and white supremacy.

The major point of Chapter 4 is that even our seemingly most secure approach to knowledge, logical positivism, cannot escape encapsulation. This position states that the only "true" knowledge is that which can be operationally defined and empirically tested. All other approaches to knowledge are not admissible, since they cannot meet the criterion of empirical testability. This leaves us with a reality image devoid of poetry, the arts, humanities, religion, etc.—perhaps an Orwellian 1984, or its alternative, a Huxleyan *Brave New World*. We are embroiled in the following paradox: if we insist on developing a reality image which is made up of only certain knowledge, we emerge with a very restricted and dehumanized world-view.

The claim of universality from the several camps has nullified the validity of an absolute status for any one truth. The fact that we are forced to several reality images rather than converging on one is regarded by many thinkers as the essence of the problem of meaning. Part I ends with Chapter 5 on a note of despair with the suggestion that the reality image of contemporary man looks something like this: "If you cannot convince me that there is some kind of knowable ultimate reality, or if you cannot convince me that there are certain absolute values by which I can live my life, I shall commit psychological suicide. That is, either convince me that there is 'one truth' or one right way of doing things, or I shall conclude that everything is meaningless and I will not try any more."

In Part II we attempt to work our way out of the nexus of nothingness. We analyze the development of meaning, pointing out that each man is responsible for his own life. Beginning with the genes which exist in the zygote at birth, we trace the limitations which are placed upon man as he interacts with the environment throughout his life span. This includes an integration of the psychology of the conditioned response, acculturation, symbolic processes, and especially, the psychology of perception. All of us are, of course, encapsulated, limited, finite; but each person has a psychobiological machinery through which he evolves a map of the nature of things. I call this map a reality image; this image or world-view represents the meaning we find in life.

Whereas in Chapter 6 I concentrate on the basis of meaning, in Chapter 7 I relate meaning to values and personality. Each man has a value hierarchy, a scale of values which he consciously or unconsciously uses as a guide or framework for ordering his behavior. The value scheme each of us adopts is a function of many things, including the elements discussed in Chapter 6 and the culture norm which is thrust upon us at a given point in time and space. Man can either remain within his "accidental" reference frame and unquestioningly accept the meaning it has to offer, or he can boldly emerge from his psycho-epistemological cocoon and broaden his reality image. The need for man to break out of his capsule is crucial, for encapsulation may well be the essence of contemporary man's spiritual emptiness.

The life of the spirit is peculiarly manifested in the way it interacts with symbols. The nature of symbol, myth, and reality is elaborated in Chapter 8. The one-to-many correspondence of the symbol is contrasted with the one-to-one correspondence of the sign. The thesis is developed that the most significant symbols, those that point to reality, are preserved for man in the form of the myth. The counterpart to this theme is the necessity for modern man to become more aware of how he is being encapsulated by semantics, traditional symbols, and contemporary myths. This chapter leans heavily on Jungian conceptions regarding unconscious processes as the source of symbolism, and on the more conscious philosophy of symbolic forms as expounded by the philosopher Ernst Cassirer. The main point of the chapter is this: the "big" myths which have come to us from the past and which will come to us in the future represent man's efforts to come to grips with ultimate reality. Thus,

we can broaden contemporary reality images by taking
the fullest possible account of the most significant images
of reality which man has provided to date.

If man wishes to gain a more inclusive world-view or
to approach ultimate reality it will be necessary for him
to break through the several cocoons within which he is
inevitably encapsulated. The first step in this process is
to recognize that he is, in fact, encapsulated. Unfortunately, this first step is the most difficult phase in the
process of becoming unencapsulated. In effect, de-encapsulation demands that we be able to get completely inside and outside of ourselves, our culture, and our time.
Perhaps we could best move toward this first step by
changing our educational philosophy so as to allow
generalist training to enrich present programs almost ex-
clusively interested in specialist training. The generalist
would then move toward meaningfulness with the authentic attitude of the existentialists while leaving behind their nihilistic tendencies, would retain the Tillich-
ian "courage to be" in the face of nothingness, take all
epistemological and value orientations into his purview,
fully explore the reality images of man which have transcended space and time in the form of myths and other
significant symbolic systems, and would emerge with an
integrated, broad-beamed reality image.

It should be noted that the unencapsulated man discussed in the last chapter of the book is not to be con-
strued as a sieve, through which everything flows, or as
an octopus, reaching out to encompass all paths to right-
eousness and reality. Rather, the unencapsulated man
has an unavoidable specific orientation, namely, that of
universalism rather than specialism. That is, he prefers
to proceed from the whole to the part rather than from
the part to the whole, from the top down rather than
from the bottom up. He wants a gestalt or total configuration into which the parts will fit, rather than con-
centration on the parts. For example, in addition to
taking into account the traditional part approach in the
history of social and political events, an approach which,
by itself, reflects over-concern for nationalism, he would
focus on a supra-nationalistic or world perspective. Such
a focus would involve histories, not of France, England,

and the United States, but rather of ideas, civilizations, and of mankind. It would put the emphasis where it belongs, on the total configurations of man-in-the-universe. Such a view would see any one nation as a very special case of universal man's struggle rather than, as now, the struggle of man against man. The unencapsulated man has an awareness of the validity and value of the many avenues to life because his approach is based on a fullness of being. In short, he claims to have a world-view or a conception of ultimate reality projected from a broad rather than a narrow reality image. And, in spite of his satisfaction with this *Weltanschauung*, he remains humble. He can remain humble because he knows that attaining complete unencapsulation is impossible, but, to the extent that he does attain it, he achieves wholeness and integration both outwardly (i.e., in his world-view) and inwardly (i.e., in degree of individuation), thereby providing an optimal setting for the release of creativity in dealing with the problem of meaning.

NOTES

1. The recent book by C. F. Wallraff, *Philosophical Theory and Psychological Fact*, Tucson: University of Arizona Press, 1961, should be consulted for a comparable view offered by a philosopher. Wallraff calls his approach "interpretationism." He says, for example, that "knowing at its best has far more in common with interpreting a text or putting together a picture puzzle than with copying a manuscript or photographing a landscape" (p. viii). He agrees with me in rejecting a restrictive, narrow view of philosophy (e.g., philosophy as logic, or as scientific only) and accepting the necessity for philosophy to deal with the totality of things in the form of interpretations of the cosmos (i.e., philosophical systems). Both Wallraff and I see the psychology of perception as basic to epistemological analysis.

Part I

The Dilemma

"At the end we have no firm ground under us, no principle to hold on to, but a suspension of thought in infinite space —without shelter in conceptual systems, without refuge in firm knowledge or faith. And even this suspended, floating structure of thought is only one metaphor of Being among others. . . ."

—KARL JASPERS

"To philosophize is to learn to die."

—MONTAIGNE

In the above two quotations we have the essence of the dilemma of man in the universe. The quote from Dr. Jaspers goes far beyond the obvious idea of relativism into the unanswerable depths. He who would push truth to the wall had better be realistic in the hard-headed sense of the scientist or even the military combat leader, and, at the same time, retain the vision of the poetic or philosophic dreamer. For truth in the all-encompassing and ultimate sense has not yet yielded to the cognitive and hypothalamic yammerings of man, and is not likely to in the future. For, as Dr. Jaspers has suggested, the best laid plans of men have, at best, yielded only a "metaphor" of the ultimate nature of things.

There are indications that many of our contemporaries have responded to the failure of our forebears to come up with ultimate answers in much the same way as a child reacts when refused a lollipop—by crying. Despite the use of the relatively more sophisticated and occasionally more obscure medium of language, they have said that life without the lollipop of ultimate answers is meaningless and therefore unbearable. It would appear that contemporary man needs to evolve a meaningful pattern of existence in face of the void and, with Montaigne, learn how to die. In Part I we take a look at man's efforts to plumb the philosophic depths, and we see that he emerges confused, encapsulated, and overwhelmed by a feeling of meaninglessness.

2

Man's Search for Reality

"The disputants I ween
Rail on in utter ignorance
Of what each other mean,
And prate about an Elephant
Not one of them has seen."

—John G. Saxe

"The complete philosopher is he who seeks not only to assign to every given object of his thought its right place in one or other of these sub-worlds, but he also seeks to determine the relation of each sub-world to the others in the total world which is."

—William James

While it is true that most of the one million species of animals possess brains of one sort or another, to our knowledge the species known as *Homo sapiens* is the only one whose brains have produced that highly complex and multi-faceted conglomeration known as modern civilization. No brain other than man's has created such things as rockets, poems, the calculus, symphonies, or the universal field theory of the universe. So far as we know man's brain is also the only brain which is aware of itself. If it is true that other forms of life are self-conscious, man is not conscious of this fact. And even if we admit to the possibility of self-awareness on the part of other forms of life, we have not yet been able to decipher the mode of expression which this self-concern might take. In man, this self-awareness has inevitably led, from generation to generation, to the asking of a profound and unyielding question: What is the meaning of man and the universe? If we put together all that we can of the jig-saw puzzle known as knowledge, what does it add up to? Does everything reduce to matter and energy? Do our observations point to an ultimate purpose? If so, what is it? Or are we just here, without

11

rhyme or reason? This quest I have called man's search for reality, and it is the purpose of this chapter to distill the essence of this search.

FOUR APPROACHES TO REALITY

In Figure 1 I have attempted to show the relationships between man, the knower, and the ultimate nature of reality by way of each of four ways of knowing. Each of

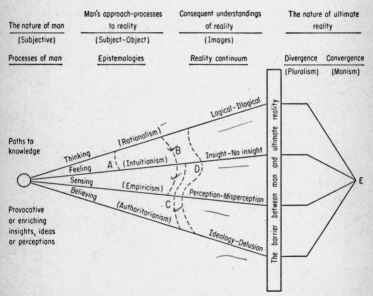

Fig. 1. The basic paths to knowledge

these ways of knowing is related to a specific psychological process in the column to the left and to a particular image[1] of reality in the column to the right. The column to the extreme right is separated from the other three columns by a barrier between man and ultimate reality. That which is testable by some criterion for knowing lies to the left of this epistemological barrier and represents what I mean by reality or truth. That which is epistemologically untestable lies to the right of the barrier and represents what I mean by ultimate reality. Note that the third column of Figure 1 allows for several reality images, each depending upon the truth criterion which is invoked. By reality image I mean one's *Weltanschauung* or world-view. This concept allows for the possibility of a sufficiently deep and broad image of reality spilling over the epistemological barrier and at least providing glimpses of ultimate reality.

Let us stay to the left of the barrier for awhile, where it is relatively safe, and briefly[2] discuss the four basic ways of knowing. I use the word "basic" because each of these ways of knowing is dependent upon psychological processes. That is, while there are more than four theories of knowledge, in the psychological sense the human organism can know only in terms of the four processes shown in Figure 1.[3] Let us take rationalism as an example of what I am trying to convey. For the sake of brevity let us refer to rationalism as that epistemological position which states that nothing is true if it is illogical. While it is true that this way of knowing includes intuitive, sensory, and other psychological components, the primary psychological process which man uses in knowing rationally is thinking. Therefore, to the extent that thinking is sharp or logical, we have been led to truth; if thinking is illogical or fuzzy, we have not been led to truth. In other words, we have a logical-illogical continuum as our criterion for knowing.

Each of the four paths to knowledge can be similarly analyzed. That is, each of the four "isms"—rationalism, intuitionism, empiricism, and authoritarianism—has a primary criterion for truth, a procedure for judging what one shall accept as true and what one shall reject as false. These criteria are indicated in the third column of Figure 1 under the label "reality continuum." Thus, empiricism is that approach to knowledge which states that we know something via sensory experience. The empiricist stays close to nature and spells "observation" with capital letters. If one can't see it, smell it, touch it, or hear it, it does not exist. We know via our sense perceptions, either in terms of our daily living or under the more controlled conditions of the experimental laboratory. If it is accurately perceived, it is true. If it is incorrectly perceived, it is illusory or false. Hence, we have a perception-misperception continuum as our criterion for this kind of knowing.

The intuitionist claims that he knows by immediate or obvious apprehension. This is a somewhat difficult doctrine of knowledge to elucidate because of the seeming necessity for using such terms as instinctive when referring to intuition, or of describing it as "a feeling" that something is so, and because of the fact that the intuitionist himself cannot clearly specify the source of his information. We speak of the intuition of a woman, the intuitiveness of a scientist or an artist, and the fact that some medical and psychological diagnosticians have intuitive "feel" for identifying certain disease syndromes. We are also well aware of the fact that intuitions have been known to be in error. This latter point is, of course, the key to the difficulty with intuition as a way of knowing. For it is the vagueness of the epistemological criterion which marks it as suspect. I think the way out of this dilemma lies in recognizing that intuitive knowledge is primarily conveyed via the symbol rather than the sign. As is more fully developed later (see Chapter 8), symbols reflect a one-to-many correspondence whereas signs reflect a one-to-one correspondence. This means that symbolic knowledge can convey multiple meanings, and intuitive awareness is, by definition, more vague than sign knowledge.

What is the psychological basis of intuition? Scientific evidence on this question is weak, although clinical psychologists have begun to look into the question.[4] In Figure 1 we suggest that it is primarily a matter of feeling. But this is merely a confusion of ignorance, cloaked behind the cliché "I have a feeling that such and such is the case." Perhaps the value in hiding behind this cliché lies in pointing to the importance of unconscious processes in intuition. That is to say, whatever lies at the psychological base of intuition, it is highly probable that this type of cognizing is occurring at a relatively low level of awareness. My guess, and that is all it can be, is that intuition is primarily dependent upon subliminal perceptual processes. Not necessarily subliminal cue reception, which is undoubtedly a special case of intuition, but rather, the non-clear perception of stimulus configurations embedded in symbolic material. This means that the usual principles of perception apply, such as the law of prägnanz and the principles of grouping (see Fig. 8, p. 90) and closure (see Fig. 9, p. 90), and that the person who is said to be intuitive is simply particularly able to pick up the appropriate stimulus configuration in spite of the fact that it is essentially hidden or disguised.

Let me use the well known phenomenon of hidden figures as a point of departure. Look at Figure 2. Some-

Fig. 2. An example of a hidden figure. If you rotate the text 90° clockwise, you will see a man on a motorcycle in the lower left quadrant of the visual field. (From N. L. Munn, Psychology, 4th Edition, Boston: Houghton Mifflin Co., 1961, p. 569)

where in this drawing is a small figure of a man on a motorcycle. You may turn the photograph upside down, sideways, etc., in an effort to locate the figure. Some individuals are capable of locating the hidden figure almost immediately. Some are incapable of finding it without assistance. In general, problems of this kind are either solved rapidly or not solved at all. I am suggesting that intuition is a perceptual phenomenon comparable to the kind of closure which occurs in identifying hidden figures.

In more general terms, I am suggesting that intuition is a matter of the immediate perception of gestalts. And I suspect that the symbol is the mediator or conveyor of the gestalt. Let us take another, more appropriate, example. How does the clinical psychologist "know" this or that about a particular client? Suppose that, as client, I am unconsciously trying to convey something to the clinician, and I do it in the usual way, via dreams and projective material. Being a sophisticated clinician, he analyzes sufficient quantities of such material and he uncovers what I was unconsciously trying to convey. The dreams and projective test results are the conveyors or mediators of my "meanings." Presumably I unconsciously project these on to the symbolic canvas, and the clinician, being an expert in "reading" symbols, picks up the stimulus configuration which I project symbolically. It is important to note that the stimulus configuration is assumed to be essentially the same for sender and receiver, or at least recognizably similar, in spite of perceptual variations in the sender (the client), the mediator (the symbol), and the receiver (the clinician). Much the same situation obtains in relationships other than the therapeutic one. For example, if it were not for a similar perceptual-symbolic backdrop between playwright and audience, the "truth" which is implicit behind the symbol system known as a play would not be capable of being conveyed. Stated another way, someone who is said to be intuitive is, in my view, not mystical, but rather, highly acute or sensitive in perceiving complex stimulus configurations.[5]

One more thought regarding the psychological processes underlying intuition. While I have suggested that it is primarily a perceptual-feeling process with strong unconscious elements, it is also possible that intuition will eventually be found to be an undifferentiated or primitive mixture of thinking and sensory processes (epistemologically, a mixture of rationalism and empiricism). While I doubt that this reduction will hold, I do think it highly likely that these processes are involved in what we call intuition. In short, whatever the eventual explanation, it is highly probable that intuition is psychologically complex, a complicated mixture of our total psychobiological equipment.

By authoritarianism we simply mean that we know on the basis of authority. If so and so said so, it must be so. The authority in question, such as a leading scientist of the time, the Pope, or a religious tome such as the Koran or the Bible, obviously commands great respect for some reason or reasons. Mortal men, such as Plato and Aristotle, have been known to reign as the true source of knowledge for centuries. Why are such authorities capable of retaining such respect? Presumably because their truth claims were viable. As soon as the truth claims of an authority fail to work the authority is cast aside.

Belief, as an approach to reality, is unavoidable on a variety of counts. The most obvious is the sheer impossibility of proceeding otherwise. If a man had to empirically test all matters of fact for himself, logically prove all items of rationality, etc., he should simply find himself overburdened. In short, practicality demands that he accept certain findings on the basis of authoritative reports from those who are supposed to know.

There is another reason that we cannot proceed without authoritarianism, and it relates directly to the thesis of this essay. The reason is that each of us is a victim of tribal conditioning. We are each encapsulated within our cultures, and from the time we were infants we have taken on a way of looking at things which was handed down to us. This includes ways of looking at reality! The Eastern stress on intuitive approaches to reality in contrast to Western empiricism is an obvious case in point.

But there is also a non-trivial (from the point of view of epistemology) reason for including authoritarianism as a legitimate approach to reality. This is because all other approaches, in the last analysis, get pushed to this approach. This unorthodox view obviously requires explanation. Here is what I mean. Each approach to reality, whether it be empiricism, rationalism, the correspondence theory of knowledge, materialism, idealism, etc., involves certain assumptions from which the view evolved. Empiricism, for example, involves the assumption that sensory inputs should receive priority in making a decision regarding truth. Rationalism, on the other hand, gives the priority to internal consistency. If we now ask for a criterion for deciding upon which assumptions to accept in evolving an image of reality, we are hard pressed to find one. Even if we could name such a criterion, we could then ask for the criterion for deciding upon criteria. In short, the question of assumptions or first principles leads to an infinite regress and forces us to the conclusion that initial assumptions are essentially given. That is to say, on theoretical grounds, any set of assumptions can be offered as a point of departure for the development of a position, and since there are no *a priori* or other definitive bases for deciding on first principles, assumptions are arbitrary or authoritarian in nature. Put another way, a belief orientation may be accepted blindly, or it may be accepted knowingly as plausible or implausible, or it may be accepted under a wide variety of conditions of awareness. Whatever the basis, in the final analysis, it is arbitrary or authoritarian.

The adequacy of the assumptions in a belief system cannot be judged by the point of origin of the assumptions, but rather, in terms of the consequences. The reality continuum, which ranges from a viable ideology to delusion (see Figure 1), suggests that the consequences can lead to psychological destruction. In other words, those belief systems which are not adaptable, or which otherwise conflict with epistemologically valid findings via other approaches, must either be abandoned or, at least, seriously reviewed in the face of all the evidence. For example, a belief system which leads me to the conclusion that the earth is, in fact, flat runs counter to the available scientific evidence regarding the earth. Because the empirical route to reality is the most powerful available route when it comes to matters of fact, it would take precedence over other findings which run counter to it. Such a belief system, or at least the portion which led to an erroneous conclusion of fact, would be very suspect and would have to be discarded.[6]

While each of these criteria provides a legitimate basis for truth, we must also note that each of these approaches is dependent upon a particular frame of reference and is therefore limited to a particular way of looking at things. For example, the intuitive religions of the East have much to offer man concerning his inner resources, self-discipline, and meditation.[7] The empirical approach to knowledge opened the door to the development of modern science, suggesting that we look at (i.e., sense) not only the physical universe, but living things and man's individual and social behavior as well. Examples of authoritarian knowledge are legion: the holy books of various religions, the dictionary, and codes of law. Mathematics is the example of rationalism *par excellence*. In mathematics we look for no phenomena other than the logical consistency of the various postulates and deductions. This has led to such abstract developments as the differential and integral calculus, matrix algebra, and topology. The fascinating thing about such purely theoretical constructs of the human mind is that they eventually turn out to be very practical models for the analysis of what we sometimes loosely refer to as the "real world" (i.e., the empirical "image"). Thus, each of these approaches has been able to provide us with provocative insights, ideas, or perceptions. When these insights and perceptions are more or less systematized, we are frequently led to believe that we are looking at "reality." But how can each of these approaches provide us with *the truth*, particularly if they do not end up with the same over-all perception of the universe? My thesis is that none of these approaches is looking at *the truth*, either individually or in combination, and further, that each approach is susceptible to encapsulation, that is, claiming to have the whole of truth or the meaning of life when one has only part of it.

PSYCHO-EPISTEMOLOGICAL ANALYSIS
OF THE SPECIAL DISCIPLINES OF KNOWLEDGE

Figure 1 shows a barrier between man and ultimate reality for the simple reason that man has no way of knowing when he will have learned all there is to know. Stated another way, it seems patently ridiculous for man, surrounded by so many obvious and glaring gaps in his knowledge, to blatantly announce that we now know all there is to know and that we are able to offer an interpretation of life which will hold for all time.[8] Despite the efforts of great thinkers to somehow circumvent the epistemological blocks involved, the only assessments open to finite man necessarily lie to the left of the barrier. Such efforts to find truth have presumably been going on since man first made his appearance in the universe, and they have slowly evolved to the current special disciplines of knowledge such as history, physics, music, religion, etc. The biases which are typical of the scientist, the artist, and other specialists are well known. In fact, it is common knowledge that modern specialism has tended to insulate one specialist from another, so that the possibilities for communication and inter-change have been minimal. In short, the "images" of truth which have been developed by various special disciplines have become so cloaked with special jargon, technical detail, and other academic in-group paraphernalia that it would be possible for all of us to be sharing the same reality image without knowing it. Worse yet, the demands of learning the special jargon and technical detail are so great that few of us even care to find out about other reality images. One of the results of a state of affairs such as this is the development of the divergent perceptions of reality depicted in Figure 3.

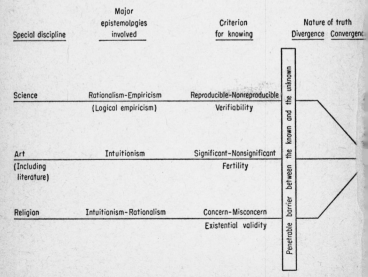

Fig. 3. Representative special disciplines of knowledge

The major item under consideration here is to compare science, art, and religion in terms of the four epistemologies described in Figure 1.[9] The most obvious conclusion to be drawn is that all three disciplines "know" via all four of the epistemologies. However, it is also clear that each discipline gives greater credence to one or more of the four ways of knowing. Let us take science as an instance. The scientist "feels," "thinks," "senses," and "believes" in his work as scientist. That is, he "knows" via rationalism, intuitionism, empiricism, and authoritarianism. However, he has learned over the centuries that, for his purpose, intuitive and authoritarian ways of knowing can be very dangerous and that they must be guarded against. He, therefore, has developed a multitude of techniques and procedures for the controlled observation of phenomena and the rational unification of these observations. He calls these procedures scientific method and scientific theory. In epistemological terms, he maximizes the rational and empirical approaches and minimizes the involvement of intuitionism and authoritarianism. Furthermore, the scientist demands that the rational and empirical findings mutually support each other. In other words, theory and fact must mesh. In the scientist's eyes theory without fact is mere speculation, and fact without theory could be something like a telephone book or a Sears and Roebuck catalogue. The crucial criterion for the admission of a finding as scientific truth is that of reproducibility. (See Figure 3.) If a given finding is verifiable in this way, it is true; if it is not, it is not admissible.

While the scientist shuns the special or unique case in the interest of arriving at a generalization, a law, or an all-inclusive theory, the artist's major consideration is the unique experience as a symbol for universal understanding. While rationalism, empiricism, and authoritarianism are all involved in varying degrees, the artist's approach to reality is primarily by way of intuitionism. Of course, his artistic creation must provide a sense of significance. If it does not do this, it will die as an artistic medium. Artistic products which have lived have met the criterion of "fertility" in one way or another. Examples of this would include the development of a new style which needed elaboration for several decades, or a new subject matter pregnant with interpretive possibilities, or the development of an entirely new form or mode of expression. Artists with whom I have discussed the problem of the nature of artistic knowledge complain of the difficulty of verbalizing the knowledge-giving qualities of art. Perhaps the analogy of "being in love" would best convey what is involved here. If asked about his condition, the love-stricken person would have great difficulty describing his condition or explaining how he knows he is "in love." The typical response is that he simply "knows." That is, he says he feels something which we denote as "love." Psycho-epistemologically, this kind of awareness seems to be primarily dependent upon one's feelings; other criteria for knowing are not as directly relevant. Perhaps I can summarize the essence of the artist's view somewhat as follows: If the artist could convey what he is trying to say with words, he would use them, rather than use the media of paint or music. In the case of the creative writer, whose medium is words, it should be pointed out that he does not use words in the same analytic fashion as the writer of philosophic or scientific tomes. Words to the professional writer are a means toward artistic ends, not mere symbols of cerebration or literal communication as in the case of the philosopher or the scientist.

Religion is undoubtedly the most difficult of the disciplines to deal with, primarily because we tend to project our own religious views into our thinking on the problem, and there are as many religious views as there are people. Perhaps I can avoid this type of confusion by using the term religion only as it relates to a special academic study. Again, all four epistemological pathways are involved, but I am taking the position that the knowledge-giving qualities of religion are dependent upon intuitionism and rationalism more than on empiricism and authoritarianism. The symbolic character of religion points up its intuitive basis, whereas its penchant for system and inclusiveness points up its rational basis. You may be surprised by my not placing authoritarianism closer to the top of the religious epistemological hierarchy. I will briefly dispose of this point by stating that I am dealing with religion in its best sense,[10] just as I have dealt with science at its best. Authoritarianism is, of course, involved in all dis-

ciplines, but I defy you to cite an acknowledged discipline
which is supported primarily by authoritarianism. Authoritarian sources, such as scientific handbooks and codes of
law, are retained as legitimate sources of knowledge because they have the weight of other types of evidence
behind them. We can state this another way. An authority as authority must be able to defend his position with
something other than incantations and mumbo jumbo.
If all he has to offer is the latter, he will eventually be
found out and discarded along with the other astrologers,
alchemists, and palm readers. What I am saying is that
religion could not have survived as a discipline of knowledge if it had been built primarily on a foundation of
authoritarianism. Unfortunately, however, there is much
superficial religion in the world and much confusion as
to the role of authority and belief.

Paul Tillich, in a small but profound book, *Dynamics
of Faith*, points to the crux of the matter when he says:

> The most ordinary misinterpretation of faith is to consider
> it an act of knowledge that has a low degree of evidence.
> . . . If this is meant, one is speaking of belief rather than of
> faith. . . . Almost all the struggles between faith an l knowl-
> edge are rooted in the wrong understanding of faith as a
> type of knowledge which has a low degree of evidence but
> is supported by religious authority. One of the worst errors
> of theology and popular religion is to make statements which
> intentionally or unintentionally contradict the structure of
> reality. Such an attitude is an expression not of faith but of
> the confusion of faith with belief.[11]

Faith, according to Tillich, "is the state of being ultimately concerned." Whatever is your ultimate concern
is your faith. It could be hot rods, money, the Communist
Party, nature spelled with capital letters, or a variety of
concepts of God. When such concerns are elevated from
their preliminary status to an ultimate level, they become
idolatrous misconcern, or judgment which was in error;
in other words, we have an example of existential or religious untruth. This is why I have advocated concern-
misconcern rather than belief-disbelief as the criterion for
admissibility to the body of religious knowledge. (See
Figure 3.) For it is not disbelief but a type of misconcern
which is revealed in novels like *Point of No Return* and

Babbitt. In these deeply symbolic novels the leading character's faith is fulfilled, but the realization of what was hoped for proves to be empty. In other words, such people believe with sufficient conviction and determination, but they invest in the "wrong" things. In terms of our analysis, this misconcern leads to a very fuzzy or, at best, a highly limited image of reality, and therefore, it has little to offer man in his search for ultimate reality. The point is that faith has to do with meaning, rather than "believing something you know ain't so."

The crucial criterion for the admission of a finding as religious truth is an existential one. That is, one's religious concern must have a significant impact on existence in order for it to yield religious truth. If such concern has a transforming effect on life, then the insights which accompany such a concern are valid. If one's ultimate concern is detrimental to life (in an historically significant sense), then the implied insights are invalid. In other words, it is absolutely essential that man invest in that concern which is really ultimate, for, in a very real sense, his life is at stake as a result of such a commitment—ultimate concern is that concern around which one builds the meaning of his existence. And as man participates in the daily business of living within the context of his ultimate concerns, those concerns which recur from generation to generation, those concerns which, in other words, continue to convey deep meaning and creativity for man, will be retained and regarded as valid. It is important to note that we avoid the idolatrous and limited concerns by the requirement of ultimacy, and that we check on ultimacy by requiring that the resultant meaning transcend particular historical situations.

In addition to ultimacy, existential validity also requires total involvement of the individual. This includes feeling as well as rationality and sensory experience. The affective involvement appears to be contrary to the concept of knowledge and therefore requires additional elaboration. As previously indicated, love is an excellent example of what we are talking about. A man and woman who love each other know primarily on a feeling or intuitive basis. Love is a felt relationship between two people which must be experienced. A man who loves his wife and children would not be aware of this relationship were it not for the affective involvement. Perhaps the evidence from the psychotherapeutic process is even clearer and more convincing. The major purpose of psychotherapy is to assist the client to attain insight into himself. This insightful or "aha" experience is a symptom of a new awareness, a reintegration of the personality, or what we might loosely term a cure. The point is that the psychoanalytic dredging of the past requires an emotional reliving before a transformation in personality can occur. A purely intellectual insight, or the verbalization of certain psychiatric terminology, does not result in the removal of neurotic or psychotic symptoms. As in the example of love, the person's existence is not affected unless there is emotion or feeling at the core of his experiences. In short, the existential criterion of knowledge accepts as true that which ultimately enhances man's existence or being and rejects as false that which diminishes his being.[12]

SCIENTIFIC AND RELIGIOUS KNOWLEDGE

Like love and psychotherapy, existential validity seems to be very powerful and convincing, but somehow slippery and difficult to pin down. Such knowledge is, of course, less exact and definite than scientific knowledge. It is, in fact, subjective since it requires a personal involvement. Scientific knowledge, on the other hand, requires the removal of personal involvement. Whereas one's existence is at stake in the religious quest, all that is at stake in the scientific quest is one's experimental design. Furthermore, in the case of the objective scientist, it really doesn't matter to what conclusions the data force him.[13] Thus, we see an interesting contrast between scientific and religious knowledge. Whereas scientific knowledge is relatively certain though lacking by comparison with religion in its significance, religious knowledge is of the utmost significance, but it lacks considerably in certainty.[14]

One of the reasons religion is lacking in certainty is that it speaks through a highly symbolic language, whereas science expresses itself literally. I am not making a plea for either scientific or symbolic language, for my position is that each discipline must invoke that medium of com-

munication which is most appropriate to its domain. Just
as it would be an error to impose the scientific criteria
for knowing upon the domain of art or religion, so it is
an error to require that poets and theologians speak the
prose language of the scientist. In my opinion, failure to
recognize the symbolic nature of the language of religion
is largely responsible for the confusion which abounds in
this area of knowledge.[15] Perhaps this point is most obvious when we contemplate the petty denominational argu-
ments concerning various literalistic interpretations of the
Bible. It is also obvious in the cavalier manner with which
certain radically positivistic scientists and philosophers
treat the problem of knowledge. If we were to accept the
view of the radical positivists, then we could find no basis
for legitimate truth in literature, art, or religion. All of
these disciplines would have to be dismissed as subjective
emotionalism, for they cannot be handled in operational
terms, nor can they be tested in the usual scientific meaning of the term "empirical."

Another reason religion lacks certainty is that it is concerned with the totality of things. The most widely accepted etymological definition of the word religion is "to
bind together." I presume any approach to life which
attempts to see it whole is bound to suffer from lack of
certainty because of the inherent impossibility of the task.
Science, on the other hand, limits itself only to those
aspects of life which are amenable to relatively precise
treatment. The theologian Martin Buber refers to the
subject matter of science as the I-it, or dealing with
things, relationships, whereas religion, he says, is concerned with I-thou, or value, relationships. Tillich makes
the contrast in terms of "controlling" and "receiving"
knowledge. Things, subject to precise analysis, can eventually be controlled, whereas non-things, which are at least
partially not subject to precise analysis, can only be received into knowledge by way of intuitive participation.
Furthermore, this involvement may not be repeatable.
That is, religious insight can emerge from a unique event,
and contrary to the scientific requirement of repeatability,
existential validity does not necessarily demand further
sampling of a given phenomenon. The scientific enterprise, on the other hand, is not concerned with the unique

event. The unique event is, in fact, somewhat distressing to the scientist, for it represents an exception to the generalization he would like to be able to formulate.

In summary, we have described scientific knowledge as dependent on rational-empirical confirmation in contrast to the existential validity of religious truth. We have suggested that while scientific truth deals with things and is therefore relatively certain, it is also relatively lacking in significance and highly partial in nature. Religious truth, on the other hand, is relatively uncertain, but it is of the greatest significance to man, for it deals with his ultimate concerns or values, and further, it attempts to come to grips with the totality of life. The scientific enterprise is objective and it moves in the direction of making generalizations. Religion, on the other hand, demands personal involvement or subjectivity, otherwise the individual would not be concerned ultimately, but only preliminarily, and furthermore, it recognizes that such individual involvement may be a unique rather than a general phenomenon. Finally, we must be very alert to the signific or literalistic language of the scientist as opposed to the symbolic language of the religionist, for a confusion of these tongues gets us immersed in complete misunderstanding of the nature of truth which is indigenous to each of these two approaches to different and complementary aspects of reality.

NOTES

1. This term was suggested by Kenneth Boulding's little book, *The Image*, Ann Arbor: The University of Michigan Press, 1956.

2. Each of these ways of knowing will be discussed in greater length in appropriate later sections. Our present concern is simply to convey the essential idea behind each of the four approaches.

3. I did not include extrasensory perception because of its doubtful status. Most psychologists take the position that the claims regarding ESP have not been adequately demonstrated. Therefore, we must suspend judgement on this matter until the evidence is more convincing.

4. See, for example, several papers by W. A. Hunt, and the recent books by P. E. Meehl, *Clinical Versus Statistical Prediction*, Minneapolis: University of Minnesota Press, 1954, and

T. R. Sarbin, R. Taft, and D. E. Bailey, *Clinical Inference and Cognitive Theory*, New York: Holt, Rinehart, and Winston, 1960.

5. The question of the trainability of such sophistication is better left undeveloped at this time since the question of whether clinicians are born or made is essentially unsettled. This is also an unresolved issue in traditional research on perception. It is the question of whether certain primitive *gestalts* are innately perceived or require prior learning (the nativism-empiricism controversy).

6. The writer included a more extended discussion of intuitionism and authoritarianism at this time because of the greater ambiguity and more questionable status of these two approaches as opposed to empiricism and rationalism. For a more complete coverage of the empirical and rational approaches, particularly as they epistemically correlate in science, see Chapter 4. The relevance of the intuitive and authoritarian approaches is explicitly extended in the discussion of symbol and myth in Chapter 8.

7. In all of the epistemological examples which are listed in the subsequent text it should be apparent that none of them is a "pure" example of the epistemology in question, and further, that these statements by no means exhaust the knowledge-giving quality of each example. For instance, the religions of the East obviously have much more to offer Western man than a few morsels on how to become more inner-directed. And, as will become clarified later, it is an obvious oversimplification to think of holy books, codes of law, and dictionaries as purely authoritarian in nature.

8. It seems intuitively obvious that this statement could be made at any point in space and time, since man, who is finite, could never be expected to take in the infinite. To be less abstruse, it is difficult for me to imagine a scientific field such as physics eventually closing up shop and going out of business because there is nothing more to learn about the physical universe. This seems to be true even on empirical grounds for the simple reason that for every question which is answered in the experimental laboratory several more are raised.

9. Any or all of the academic disciplines could be similarly analyzed. These particular three were chosen because they best represent the full gamut of knowledge. That is, the term science covers the natural and social sciences, the term art is meant to include all the fine arts—music, drama, literature, etc.—and religion is representative of what is known as the humanities. The discipline of philosophy is perhaps not adequately repre-

sented by any one of these, although it is most akin to religion. An abbreviated epistemological analysis of philosophy would indicate that it is essentially rational.

10. By "best" I mean symbolic or non-literalistic as opposed to signific or literalistic. This point is amplified more fully in later sections, especially in Chapter 8.

11. Paul Tillich, *Dynamics of Faith,* New York: Harper & Bros., 1957, pp. 31-34.

12. The writer recognizes the fact that the concept of existential validity requires more rigorous explication. This task is presently underway under the title "Psychology, Epistemology, and Existential Validity."

13. I trust it is clear that this statement refers to a matter of principle in the application of a truth criterion. As a human being, seriously involved in his work, the scientist has a personal stake in the outcome of his investigations, of course. But, in principle, he tries to apply the doctrine of no invested interest in the analysis of his data. If he fails to do this, his results will not be empirically confirmable.

14. Here I am speaking of certainty in terms of epistemological validity rather than psychological certainty. The fact that a person might be willing to die in the name of religious conviction, therefore, is irrelevant. Such a person manifests the ultimate in subjective certainty, but such conviction, in and of itself, does not necessarily mean that it carries epistemological validity with it. My position on the relationship between epistemology and religious conviction has been developed in this section under the rubric of existential validity, the implication being that transformation in the quality of existence is the crucial requirement, not subjective certainty.

15. A more extended discussion of the symbol as it is related to meaning and knowledge will be found in Chapters 4 and 8.

3

The Problem of Encapsulation*

"*Archetypes come to the fore again and again in history, always presuming at each moment of history that the particular form in which they find themselves is the only one that is 'true' and 'eternal.'*"

—Ira Progoff

"*If the doors of perception were cleansed, everything would appear to man as it is, infinite. For man has closed himself up till he sees all things through the narrow chinks of his cavern.*"

—William Blake

In the previous chapter we described four ways of knowing and three special disciplines of knowledge. We concluded that each of these approaches has been able to provide us with provocative insights, ideas, or perceptions, but that none of them, either individually or in combination, has been able to lead us to "the truth" in the sense of ultimate reality. Further, we have suggested that man, in his attempt to come to grips with ultimate reality, cannot do so because he is limited, finite; in short, because he is encapsulated.

What do we mean by encapsulation? In general, we mean claiming to have all of the truth when one only has part of it. We mean claiming to have truth without being sufficiently aware of the limitations of one's approach to truth. We mean looking at life partially, but issuing statements concerning the wholeness of living. In its most important sense the term "encapsulation" refers to projecting a knowledge of ultimate reality from the perceptual framework of a limited reality image. It will be recalled that in Chapter 2 we made a distinction between two types of reality: (1) finite reality, or our best—

* Reprinted from the *Journal of Existential Psychiatry*, 1961, *1*, 426-440, by permission of Libra Publishers, Inc., 1133 Broadway, New York 10, N. Y.

estimate of the nature of things and (2) ultimate reality, or the final essence of things. More precisely, we referred to finite reality as epistemologically testable (i.e., to the left of the barrier in Figure 1) and to ultimate reality as being epistemologically untestable (to the right of the barrier in Figure 1). Further, we discussed reality image as it relates to each of these conceptions of reality. That is, if by reality image we mean one's perception of what is real or true, we suggested that some individuals, such as mystics, claim to have an image of ultimate reality, whereas other individuals confine their reality image to the finite reality on the left side of the epistemological barrier. In this chapter we wish to discuss the problem of encapsulation as it relates to both finite reality and ultimate reality. When one's reality image is projected across the epistemological barrier, we shall be speaking of encapsulation in the ultimate sense. On the other hand, we shall also consider the case of finite encapsulation, that is, the case of confining one's reality image to the left side of the barrier.

ENCAPSULATION AND ULTIMATE REALITY

Let us consider the former case first, that is, the case of pronouncing "the truth," the final essence of things, from the perceptual framework of a limited reality image. Artists, scientists, mystics, empiricists, rationalists, etc., have all made such pronouncements and are therefore guilty of encapsulation. In fact, the taking of absolutistic stands from the base of epistemological relativism lies at the core of our present confusion. Examples of this are legion. We see it in the denominational religionist who cannot rest unless he forces his way of seeing things upon the rest of humanity. We see it in highly nationalistic countries, artists of certain schools of thought, self-pronounced prophets, and other special interest groups. We see it in academic circles among our highly specialist-oriented colleagues. Each specialist has *the* route to "really ultimate truth," and if you want to be saved, all you have to do is get the word from him. And we see it among great philosophers who have tried for centuries to penetrate the epistemological barrier of Figure 1 with metaphysical guesses as to what might lie beyond it. We can place these efforts into essentially two categories, monistic guesses and pluralistic guesses. The materialistic monist, for example, states that everything ultimately reduces to matter or energy. Berkeley argued that everything reduces to mind and ideas. Pantheists say that God is everywhere; and so it goes. What do we have here? Very simply and briefly, we have an example of an insight about one aspect of reality which is overgeneralized and pronounced to the world as the essence of everything. How does Berkeley know that everything reduces to mind? Or how do the materialists know that everything reduces to matter or energy? How did they leap the epistemological wall and gain their insight, and how can they both be right? At this point, the dualists come onto the scene. They point out that neither the materialist nor the mentalist is correct, that instead, things reduce to mind *and* matter. They suggest that mental phenomena are not reducible to transformations of energy, and further, that material events cannot be accounted for as manifestations of some kind of underlying spirit.

This dualistic position is widely prevalent in contemporary Western culture, and is obviously manifested in such terms as mind-body, psychosomatic, or psychophysiological. We talk about the brain and neurons in one breath and mental tests and intelligence in the next breath, but we do not know how to discuss such matters in a truly integrated or non-dualistic fashion. Physicalistic monists see mental events as epi-phenomena or as illusory. They are convinced that all things mental are basically understandable in terms of underlying energy exchanges. The argument on the other side, however, is convincing in its claim that complex behavioral events can only be understood in terms of organizational principles which transcend purely reductionistic atomic conceptualizations. Descartes, who initiated the mind-object cleavage, also worried about the problem of interaction of mind and body, particularly within the human organism. He was unable to come up with a solution, merely suggesting that the pineal gland, an endocrine structure at the base of the brain, was the link between the mental and the physical. Other pluralists have not been satisfied with twoness;

they have suggested that the great diversity of the universe requires a large number of categories, perhaps three, four, or five. For example, there is the material pluralism of Empedocles in which earth, air, fire, and water were offered as the basic elements of the universe. The Greeks professed spiritual pluralism, that is, polytheism, in which they specified a variety of gods as the essence of things. Contemporary knowledge suggests that the Greeks, while in error in empirical details, were right in positing a pluralistic position, as evidenced by the one hundred or so basic elements of matter and the forty or fifty components of intelligence, but we are still no closer to a solution to the riddle of whether matter is reducible to mind, vice versa, or whether some kind of psychophysical dualism is necessary.

These two kinds of ultimate reality, monistic and pluralistic, are provided for in Figure 1. If the several epistemological approaches remained divergent on the other side of the barrier, then ultimate reality would, in fact, be pluralistic. But if all these approaches were mere manifestations of one underlying reality, then they would converge to the right of the barrier, and we would have "the truth," a monism of some sort. My position is that *we do not know* whether the nature of ultimate reality is convergent or divergent for the simple reason that we have no adequate procedure for making such an assessment. And further, I am saying that those who make pronouncements about the ultimate nature of things are doing just that—making pronouncements. For they are just as limited as the rest of us, and they have no special short-cuts to truth. Until visionaries, mystics, and other claimants to ultimate truth can make their epistemological route clearer to competent investigators, we shall have to conclude that such men are encapsulated reality seekers along with the rest of us. The radical rationalist finds justifiable and proper insights along the reality continuum of reason and places relatively minimal emphasis on the sensory of empirical approach to truth. The radical materialist, on the other hand, is primarily empirical; he confines himself to what he can sense, and so he blows up his empirical reality image beyond proper proportions, knowingly or unknowingly vaults the epistemological barrier, and boldly proclaims that all is matter. And the only difference between such monorail reality seekers and the pluralists is that the pluralists at least have the sense to ride more than one reality rail. But apparently they think themselves immune to finitude, for they also commit the error of pronouncing ultimates from a highly limited awareness of the totality of things. I suggest that it requires ultimate reality in order to be aware of ultimate reality, and that, therefore, such infinite and all-encompassing awareness is not available to finite, limited man.[1]

ENCAPSULATION AND FINITE REALITY

But what of the situation of coming to grips with finite reality? If man cannot grasp the ultimate, can he at least deal with finite reality? As we might expect, man does much better here, not because he is any less encapsulated, but simply because he sets himself a more modest goal. That is, as long as we stay to the left of the barrier we are confining ourselves to a finite and knowable universe. Note, however, that the effort is still made from the perspective of a limited reality image. That is, we still have to contend with the monorail reality seeker who claims a broader truth than his limited reality image entitles him to. We are still confronted with overgeneralization, distortion, and finitude. We are still up against *one* approach to reality which is promoted as *the* approach to reality. Such myopia is the most fundamental sense in which man is encapsulated in his attempt to evolve a world-view or reality image of finite reality. While the major limitation in the case of the reality image which attempts to encompass ultimate reality is that man is not omniscient, the major limitation in the case of the reality image which attempts to encompass finite reality is the more human limitation of failing to make optimal use of the various approaches which are available. The person who approaches reality by only one epistemological route is not making the most of his basic psychobiological equipment, and this limitation simply does not provide him with a broad enough base from which to project a world-view. Such world-views can vary all the way from the relatively broad perspective of the artist or the scientist down to the trivial perspective of the bigoted and the prejudiced. Since this type of encapsulation deals with a finite universe, the very real finitude of possible "reality images" comes to mind more readily in this connection than it does when one thinks of the type of encapsulation which is concerned with ultimate reality. In an extreme case of encapsulation, for example, the world-view or *Weltanschauung* would approach or equal *zero*. Consider, for instance, the case of a person of very low I.Q. whose conception of reality is limited to certain very specific, discrete, concrete things such as his shoe, a table, a chair, etc. An individual with even lower I.Q., say that equal to an idiot or imbecile, would be little more than a vegetable, and in a very real sense, the *Weltanschauung* of such an organism would actually approach zero.

Similarly the views of possibly more intelligent, but variously prejudiced individuals, would also represent people of very limited world-views. The reduction in ambiguity which would follow if prejudiced notions were true is obvious. If the "true" social structure were in fact a communal one, and if all Negroes were in fact stupid, and if Americans were always right, then the realities of the world would move into a whole series of black and white dichotomies with all in-between shades of gray removed. The realities in such an image are very simple and clear-cut, with a consequent reduction concerning the ambiguities of life. What one "ought to do" is, then, very simple and obvious to the prejudiced mind. Thus, we have loud screams about what ought to be done in the name of "truth" from such highly encapsulated individuals as America firsters, fascists, rabid nationalists from a variety of countries, racists, cultists, and psychotics. Perhaps the most obvious contemporary example of proselyting in the name of truth is evident in the international aggressiveness of Soviet Russia. Dr. Kirby Page, a long-time student of Russia and a visitor there in the summer of 1957, reported in a lecture at the University of Redlands in 1958 shortly before his death that it is just this proselyting fervor which is the major motivation behind Soviet aggressiveness. He says the Communists are convinced they have "the right way," the "real" truth, and they are convinced that the rest of us need this kind of medicine, and, if necessary, they will force it upon us for our own good.

I see great similarities between such firmly entrenched and staunchly defended views and those views held by cultists and psychotics. Both cultist and psychotic, for example, are just as convinced of the reality and the unusual insightfulness of their perceptions. The difference between the cultist and the psychotic is that the cultist manages to stay on the right side of everyday empirical reality, and so we do not force him into an institution, but his "reality image" is clearly distorted and rigid by all other counts, as is the "reality image" of the psychotic. Such men are perhaps the most obvious examples of encapsulation, since they do not get beyond their externally encapsulating pressures, and further, they fail completely to get outside their internally encapsulating pressures as well. The cultist and the psychotic do not necessarily find meaninglessness in their "reality images"; they simply have "reality images" that are so unique that very few other individuals are able to share them. This point brings out one of the reasons we need at least a degree of the security which comes from conformity behavior. If we are able to "fit in" with others, it suggests that we at least see things as others do, and it is indicative of the fact that we still have our sanity.

WHY WE ARE ALL ENCAPSULATED

Questions of this kind move us into a consideration of the conditions which lead to encapsulation. That is, what accounts for encapsulation? And why are some men more encapsulated than others? Let us begin by pointing out the obvious fact that all of us are encapsulated by definition, that is, by virtue of being men. The thought that men are highly limited creatures should not come as a shock. Let us examine the evidence. Man enters the world with the imprint of genes from his ancestors and the foetal environment of his mother. As a result of a highly complex interaction of environmental and constitutional forces, involving such things as conditioning, acculturation, and maturation, a set of meanings[2] begins to emerge in the growing child and the latent adult. In short, the person develops a way of looking at the world—he develops a reality image.

However, men have their limitations in looking at reality. They do not hear sound frequencies outside the range of 20 to 20,000 cycles per second, for example. They are not very accurate in localizing the source of sounds. Man's tactual sensitivity is none too sharp, and his ability to discriminate a variety of smells and tastes is equally poor. He is able to see only the tiniest segment of the total range of wavelengths of light. The total light spectrum extends from the cosmic rays (10 trillionths of an inch) at the short wavelength end to the long waves of radio (measured in miles) at the other end. The human eye is only capable of responding to those wavelengths which vary from 380 millionths of a millimeter to 760 millionths of a millimeter. This represents 1/70 of the total light spectrum! Men are also limited in their ability to learn and to think.

Many individuals cannot learn higher mathematics, some are baffled by poetry, memories are rarely prodigious. Have someone recite eight or ten digits one second apart, and then try to recite them back. Now try to repeat the digits in reverse order. How many married men of 35 can remember the names of their first three or five girl friends? Forgetting is much more rapid than learning. One of the major reasons the college professor is so proficient in his special subject is that he has been teaching it for 25 years, after spending 8 or 10 years to get his Ph.D. The only things that are readily retained are those that have been learned and relearned. And most men are not capable of broad and abstract thinking. How many men are philosophers in the professional sense? How many scientists think in the broad perspectives of an Einstein? Most scientists consider themselves fortunate if they can make one honest contribution to knowledge during a lifetime.

Furthermore, man's rationality is limited by his irrationality. That is, man's ability to involve his cortex as he navigates through life is inhibited by the overpowering effect of his hypothalamus. This is another way of saying that emotional and unconscious processes frequently functionally decorticate thinking of rational man. The result of decortication is lack of ability to think, and there are many indications that man is not as much of a thinking organism as philosophers consider him. The psychotherapist's couch is overburdened with the results of the conflict between hypothalamic and cortical confusions in man's brain. The fact of the matter is that we are so ignorant about unconscious processes and what motivates men that we cannot even estimate very intelligently to what extent irrationality and rationality are characteristic of man.

Man's imagination is even limited. Before the Copernican revolution it was difficult to imagine a world in terms other than flat. The universe was seen as a three-story building with heaven on the top floor, the earth as the ground floor, and hell as the basement. Our imaginations are similarly staggered by the prospects of outer space! The idea of a boundless universe, for example, is essentially incomprehensible to us.

In addition to encapsulating forces which have their impact on the individual at the psychobiological level, there are also forceful limiting conditions which affect man's conceptualizing at the psycho-cultural level. The importance of cultural and social factors as determinants of the way men think and behave have been well documented by extensive field studies on primitive societies. The studies of the cultural anthropologists clearly showed that these social expressions were consciously and unconsciously learned and that they were passed on to the individual by way of the culture and subcultures. In one cultural group perhaps aggressiveness would be played up as a desirable social norm; in another culture just the opposite would be the case. Ruth Benedict's book *Patterns of Culture*[3] is a well written account of the importance of these cultural differences in the determination of the "normal" personality of three very different peoples, the Pueblo Indians of New Mexico, the Kwakiutls of the Northwest, and the Dobuans of New Guinea. The Pueblos are described as being essentially self-effacing, the Kwakiutls as being concerned with glorification to the point of megalomania, and the Dobuans as being a treacherous, and even murderous, lot.

The importance of cultural relativism to the understanding of human behavior cannot be overestimated.

And, just as large groups, such as nations, or Western or Eastern civilizations, set the patterns by which people live, so do various subcultures and subparts of the culture, serve as important determinants of behavior. One of the most important of these subpart determinants is that of language. In a brilliant series of essays which were recently collected and edited in book form by J. B. Carroll, the late B. L. Whorf[4] has assembled both theoretical and empirical data to show that language has similarly important effects. In fact, the Whorfian hypothesis states that the structure of language sets limitations on our thought processes, thereby determining how we see the world around us. He shows, for example, that the Hopi Indians have an entirely different conception of time than does the European. In effect, the Hopi sees time as cyclic rather than continuous, and this structure of thought is directly traceable to the no-tense Hopi verb forms in contrast to the three-tense European verb form. Thus, tomorrow for the Hopi does not lie in the future, but rather, it represents the reappearance of light in the light-dark circle. Whorf has documented his thesis at great length and clearly shows that the various segments of a language impose "cognitive modes" on the way man categorizes his world perceptually or conceptually. The fact that this type of limitation is just as "real" as that of human audition (i.e., 20 to 20,000 cycles per second) and vision (380 to 760 millionths of a millimeter) is evident in the following quotation from Whorf.[5]

> And every language is a vast pattern-system, different from others, in which are culturally ordained the forms and categories by which the personality not only communicates, but also analyzes nature, notices or neglects types of relationships and phenomena, channels his reasoning, and builds the house of his consciousness. . . .
> . . . This shows that word-coining is no act of unfettered imagination, even in the wildest flights of nonsense, but a strict use of already patterned materials. If asked to invent forms not already prefigured in the patternment of his language, the speaker is negative in the same manner as if asked to make fried eggs without the eggs! . . .
> . . . Thinking also follows a network of tracks laid down in the given language, an organization which may concentrate systematically upon certain phases of reality, certain aspects

of intelligence, and may systematically discard others featured by other languages."

In the process of studying Whorf's work an important insight concerning the limitations of rational thought struck me as a legitimate outgrowth of his thinking on psycholinguistics. Carroll [6] points out that there are over 2,000 different language systems. It is also general knowledge that there are at least several hundred mathematical systems. Each system, whether it be linguistic or mathematical, has certain given figures and postulates, syntax, or rules as to how to play the game. Within the limitations of the original "givens," the system "works" quite well. But it is obvious that matrix algebra, where $AB \neq BA$, is quite a different way of looking at things than classical algebra, where $ab = ba$. Similarly, there are certain words which cannot be translated into certain other languages. This is notoriously true for translating German into English, for example, where such words as "gestalt" get carried over into the English directly because of the essential untranslatability of the German word. In short, any rational system is, by definition, limited to handling only that portion of the totality of the rational which its presuppositions will permit. It is in this sense that Bertrand Russell [7] recently proclaimed that he thought of mathematics as essentially an empty tautology and therefore not worthy of prolonged deliberation. The point is that language *is* a rational system; it is a way of conceptualizing about one's experience. But, any given language is simply *one* way to come to terms with life.

A major difference between language as a rational scheme and mathematics as a rational scheme lies in the degree of consciousness attending its development. While the origins of the simpler mathematical systems are in some cases lost in antiquity, it is clear that highly trained mathematicians and logicians, such as Bertrand Russell, consciously create such systems and that they are quite aware of the artificiality of what they have created. Language, on the other hand, is almost entirely an unconscious affair. We still have no convincing theory concerning the origin of language. And, in general, we are simply not aware of the ways it encapsulates our thought. Whorf is quite aware of this point, and he indicates that this unconscious ignorance is one of the major reasons why we, especially Western man, are so cocksure of our conception of reality.

> The individual is utterly unaware of this organization and is constrained completely within its unbreakable bonds. . . . They are as unaware of the beautiful and inexorable systems that control them as a cowherd is of cosmic rays. . . . Hopi can have verbs without subjects, and this gives to that language power as a logical system for understanding certain aspects of the cosmos. Scientific language, being founded on western Indo-European and not on Hopi, does as we do, sees sometimes actions and forces where there may be only states. For do you not conceive it possible that scientists . . . project the linguistic patterns of a particular type of language upon the universe, and *see* them there, rendered visible on the very face of nature? *A change in language can transform our appreciation of The Cosmos.* [Italics mine— J.R.R.]

> All this is typical of the way the lower personal mind, caught in a vaster world inscrutable to its methods, uses its strange gift of language to weave the web of Maya or illusion, to make a provisional analysis of reality and then regard it as final. Western culture has gone farthest here, farthest in determined thoroughness of provisional analysis, and farthest in determination to regard it as final. The commitment to illusion has been sealed in western Indo-European language. . . .[8]

Thus, language encapsulation leads directly to thought encapsulation at the cosmic level, which means that we are again unable to escape the cosmic womb. For not only are our imaginations, our space ships, and our telescopes too feeble to encompass the outer reaches of space, but so is our language. Our ability to conceptualize, then, is clearly limited by the presuppositions of our culture and our times. The *Zeitgeist* also limits the ways in which it is permissible to think. Witness Galileo, who bucked the *Zeitgeist* and was forced to recant. And consider the usually brutal history which accompanies practically any revolutionary idea. As ingenious as man is, with his highly facile, flexible brain, he is limited in his ability to understand the world around him and his world within. Each individual comes to a reality image in his own unique fashion—in terms of his own limitations and strengths. For example, if we add to the fact of limited hearing the additional fact that a particular man may have poor pitch discrimination, or that another man may have "perfect pitch discrimination," and if we multiply this psycho-biological individuality by some unknown astronomical figure, it strikes me as amazing that we are able to share individual "reality images" at all! However, different men, living in different places at different times, have found that certain "reality images" have been more or less successful in dealing with the problems of life. Such viable images, shared by more and more men, eventually attain the status of the philosophy of a culture, a great religious system, a philosophic position, or the way of life of an epoch. Such a grand scheme, the broadest possible reality image of a people, in spite of its all-inclusiveness, is bound to find itself pushed to the big questions for which it doesn't really have answers, including the question of ultimate reality. What usually happens at this juncture? Perhaps primarily because of the demands which a people make on themselves for *the* answers, we find such an image being projected across the barriers of ignorance and finitude into the realm of the ultimate. In the emotional wake of having come upon *the truth*, the proponents are unfortunately not aware of the metaphysical leap they have performed. They become so immersed with the possibilities and the obvious truth of what they have to offer that they are literally unaware of their encapsulation. Man seems to insist on pursuing this "pot of gold at the end of the rainbow" kind of thing in all places, at all times, and in all walks of life. He seems to demand that there is such a thing as a best and only system of ethics, a best and only political state, a best and only philosophic system, and a best and only truth. Behind this concern I see a variety of value orientations or presuppositions, each screaming for absolute status, and each demanding that man therefore live accordingly. Medieval man, for example, got his reality image primarily from the church, with relatively little contribution from science. The situation is essentially reversed in the case of 20th-century man.

By what criteria can a decision be reached concerning which approach results in a clearer perception of ultimate reality? There are none, for one would have to know the nature of ultimate reality in order to assess whether or not a given image of reality was closer to it than another image. And who is to say whether man would, in fact, be more secure if he were eventually able to close in on ultimate reality? Apparently he has been convinced that knowledge of ultimate reality would provide him with optimal control of himself and everything in his environment, thereby minimizing the ambiguity of life. I suggest that just the opposite would be more likely. I suggest that the great adventure of life resides in the search for ultimates, but not the attainment of them. Our history books are filled with the testimony of what happens to a people when they become convinced they have *the truth*. They perish. And they perish because their reality image becomes frozen. After all, if you have come to the essence of things, you have reached the pot of gold at the end of the rainbow and there is no more need to search.

On the other hand, there is an equally overwhelming spiritual malaise which accompanies solipsism, the philosophic view that there is no truth. Such a view constitutes psychological suicide, for it literally removes the possibility for reliable contact between self and the outside world. Psychologically, this kind of philosophic adjustment is a reaction-formation to absolutism. It says, "Since there are no *absolute* truths, it follows that there are *no* truths." This view has been briefly presented in order to make the point that the position of "*no* truth" is at least as preposterous as the position of "*the* truth." It follows, therefore, that some kind of commitment to reality is inevitable, or at least psychologically necessary. Our plea is that this commitment occur in such a way as to enable the psyche to remain open; in short, our plea is for commitment without encapsulation.

The search for ultimate reality, then, is a natural and necessary part of man's being. We need to realize that this kind of concern is part of what it means to be human. We also need to realize, however, that while some kind of commitment is inevitable, a final answer to this question can never be given, for man is limited, he is finite;

he can never be expected to know all. In short, he is encapsulated, and for him to *know* the infinite is impossible by definition.

NOTES

1. The error in most institutionalized religions has been that of thinking they could *know* ultimate reality. At this point Tillich helps us greatly, for he points out that religion has to do with ultimate *concern* rather than ultimate *knowledge*.

2. A more complete treatment of the factors which account for meaning is given in Chapter 6.

3. Ruth Benedict, *Patterns of Culture*, New York: Houghton Mifflin Co., 1934.

4. B. L. Whorf, Language, Mind and Reality, *The Theosophist*, Vol. LXIII, January and April 1942. In *Language, Thought and Reality*, Cambridge: M.I.T. Press, 1956.

5. *Ibid.*, pp. 252 and 256.

6. J. B. Carroll, *A Study of Language*, Cambridge: Harvard University Press, 1953.

7. Bertrand Russell, *My Philosophical Development*, New York: Simon and Schuster, 1959.

8. Whorf, *op. cit.*, pp. 256, 257, and 263.

4

The Encapsulation of Science and Logical Positivism[1]

"Whereof one cannot speak, thereof one must be silent"

—Ludwig Wittgenstein

"If I had my life to live over again, I would have made it a rule to read some poetry and listen to some music at least every week. . . . The loss of these tastes is a loss of happiness, and may possibly be injurious to the intellect, and more probably to the moral character, by enfeebling the emotional part of our nature."

—Charles Darwin

"The knowledge of science fails in the face of all ultimate questions."

—Karl Jaspers

The development of science as an approach to truth is a relatively recent occurrence when seen against the backdrop of man's total history. While it is true that rudimentary sciences have existed since man's beginnings in the form of number systems and the highly developed techniques and skills of craftsmen of various sorts, science in the modern sense did not begin until the Renaissance. There was, of course, science of a sort at the height of the Greek civilization in the 3rd, 4th, and 5th centuries B.C. However, except for certain taxonomic and mild observational forays on the part of an occasional Aristotle or Archimedes, Greek science was essentially rationalistic or philosophic. But during the 14th and 15th centuries men began to look around with more open eyes and minds and to speak out with more open mouths and hearts. They explored faraway places, such as the Western Hemisphere. And they pronounced new theories concerning the nature of the celestial universe, and the position of man and earth in that universe. In short, they broke out of their earth-bound, church-bound capsule and began to move from a closed to an open universe.[2]

The new attitude of seeing for one's self spread briskly, and the released creativity mushroomed into an impressive array of scientific invention and observation. In 1593 Galileo invented the thermometer, in 1608 a Dutchman invented the telescope, and in 1643 the barometer was developed. Gilbert reported observations on magnetism in the early 1600's, Kepler pronounced the laws of planetary motion around 1610, and Harvey discovered the circulation of the blood around 1630. Newton burst upon the scene around 1665 and dominated it until his death. The first scientific society (The Royal Society) was founded in England in 1660, and the *Philosophical Transactions* of The Royal Society was published in 1665. The publication of the modern scientific journal, however, did not come upon the scene until the end of the 18th century. These early developments were primarily in the physical sciences, especially those of astronomy and physics. But as scientists met with more and more success, their methods were applied to more and more fields, so that by the beginning of the 20th century man had finally worked around to himself again with the emergence of the scientific approach to his own behavior. A very brief summary suggests that it would be reasonable to think of the 15th century as one of geographical exploration, the 16th and 17th centuries as those of exploration in the physical sciences, the 18th and 19th as marking the emergence of the biological sciences, and the 20th century as the age of psychological or behavioral science.

In the history of scientific thought, particularly in the modern period from around 1500 to the present day, there have been two major philosophical epistemologies relevant to the history of science: rationalism and empiricism. While both traditions can be traced to antiquity, the rationalist trend has dominated all thought from the beginning, particularly since the time of the Greeks. Since the Renaissance, however, the empiricist tradition has gained tremendous momentum, and it may be said to be dominant on the contemporary science scene.

A SYNTHESIS OF SCIENTIFIC METHODS
OF OBSERVATION

Let us take a closer look at empiricism as it relates to the scientific enterprise. It will be recalled that the empiricist is one who approaches reality via his sensory perceptions. Such a man feels that something is "really" real if he can either see it, hear it, touch it, or smell it. He is essentially hard-headed and literalistic, and his ultimate goal is to accumulate what he calls "facts." Scientists have found that the business of wresting facts from nature is a difficult and tricky business, primarily because of limitations of the observer. So, over the centuries he has devised a variety of procedures or methods, commonly misunderstood as *the scientific method,* for making empirical observations. These observations are concerned with maximizing the objectivity with which the observation is made. The interest in objective observations means the scientist must consider ways of introducing "control" over what he observes and, at the same time, minimally distort "nature." "Control" means the ability to isolate and assess the effect of variables which are relevant to what is being observed. Common sense or everyday observations lack control completely and cannot lead to scientific observations because of the complete omission of orderliness or plan in that which is to be observed. Field observations distort nature the least (i.e., not artificial, natural), but they involve the least degree of control. Therefore the consequent knowledge of operating variables is somewhat speculative, and predictability is highly questionable. Clinical observations are based on nature's accidents and also suffer from lack of controlled observation. Because of these factors many observations are required before clear-cut factual conclusions can be reached. Here the final effect is clearly observable, but the cause or causes can only be guessed at—hence, the well known confusion and the artistic component of any clinical practice such as medicine or psychology. It is, of course, true that such practitioners, while they use the results of science, are not primarily scientists, certainly not in the more precise sense of being observers of contrived and controlled events. Note, however, that in spite of the lack of control, the clinician is an observer, and to the extent that his observations are repeatable and generalizable, he is a scientist. Freud, a clinician, enjoys confused status as a scientist because, in spite of his great psychological insights and his unquestioned genius for speculative thought, much of what he has proposed remains empirically unconfirmed and, in many cases, is actually unconfirmable. As will be developed more fully later, much Freudian thought is scientifically unconfirmable because there is no way to translate his thought into procedures which will provide the necessary empirical tests.

The scientist has been most ingenious in devising ways and means of improving on common sense in making his observations. This ingenuity is summarized in Table 1, which can serve as a guide as we continue our exposition of the scientist's methods of observation. We have already covered the first three types of observation, which have been labeled (column 2) common sense, naturalistic, and case study. The next three types of observation represent the laboratory or near-laboratory situation wherein the scientist, in one way or another, is able to make reasonably accurate assessments of the contribution of each variable to the observed effect. I said in one way or another because in the case of a psychological test, for example (see *Semi-laboratory observations*), the way is essentially statistical, whereas in the case of astronomical observations (see *Predicted observations in nature*), while strictly speaking not a laboratory experiment, the relevant variables are so well known that, in effect, nature provides a "controlled experiment" for the informed man. The optimum condition for the controlled observation is, of course, the laboratory experiment, for this provides the observer with observations or measurements which are repeatable within very small degrees of error.

There are innumerable ways to set up a "controlled" observation. The details of the technique, procedure, instrumentation, measurement, etc., depend upon what is being observed and the scientist's conception of the best way to get at it. The general term which describes this wide variety of observations is "experimental designs." The classical experimental design is known as the single variable design; it is what most people mean when they speak of *the* scientific method. This design was brought into science with the Renaissance and has been the major experimental approach of science until the 20th century. The major components of the single-variable design are the dependent variable, the independent variable, the careful ignoring of irrelevant variables (so as to avoid a neurotic breakdown of the experimental scientist who is never sure about which variables to carefully control and which ones can be ignored), and the careful "control" of all other relevant variables. When properly conducted and if the results are positive, such a design leads to what has been referred to as an "if-then" statement. That is, *if* such and such is the case, *then* such and such will happen. (For example, *if* you properly mix two parts of hydrogen with one part of oxygen, *then* water will be formed.) The *then* part of the statement represents the dependent variable, whose effects are *dependent* upon how the experimenter manipulates the *independent* (or *if*) variable. This can be simply shown as in Figure 4.

Independent variable (if) —————————➤ (then) Dependent variable

Fig. 4. The single variable experimental design

The extension of scientific observations to life processes, behavioral phenomena, and social events pointed up the fact that the classical single-variable experimental design was not always appropriate to scientific problem-solving in these fields. While it should be made clear that single-variable experiments have been conducted in all of these newer scientific areas, experimentalists in these fields found it necessary to devise more appropriate ways of designing experiments or controlling observations. These 20th-century experimental designs are called multiple-variable designs because they allow for the "controlled" observation of more than one variable at a time. They are more appropriate designs for many problems in

TABLE 1

A Synthesis of Scientific Methods of Observation

Type of Observation	Brief Description of Type of Observation	Examples of Types of Observation	Conditions of Observation
Observation in daily life	Common sense	See sky, trees, animals, reflect on one's thoughts	Relatively undirected, uninformed observing; observation relatively random
Observation in the field	Naturalistic	Bird watching; observing a riot; watching social behavior of monkeys in natural habitat	Man knows "what to look for" in his observing; he selects what he will see
Observation in the clinic	Case study	Medical, psychological clinics	Man can "recognize" what the accidents and forces of nature randomly present to the clinician
Semi-laboratory observations	"Standardized" conditions of observation	Psychological test; observation dome	Man specifies the conditions but does not "control" the variables, the variables are free to vary under the specified conditions
Predicted observation in nature (field or clinic)	Naturalistic experiment	Astronomical observation of position at a given time	Nature provides "controlled" experiment for the informed man
Laboratory observations	Experiments	Speed of sound or light	Man artificially "controls" relevant variables in the laboratory

the non-physical sciences because of the greater complexity of phenomena in these areas.

There are two large categories of multiple-variable design, the analysis of variance designs and the factor analysis designs. The analysis of variance designs are concerned with assessing the effects of many independent variables on a particular dependent variable, as shown in Figure 5. This procedure allows the experimentalist to effect a great deal of time saving by telescoping many single-variable experiments into one complex experimental setting. It also allows for the assessment of interaction

TABLE 1 (*Continued*)

Equipment and Other Tool Aids in Observing	Degree of "Control" of Observation	Relative Scientific Validity of Knowledge Gained (Repeatability)	Comments
None	Completely uncontrolled	Completely speculative	Can lead to "hunches" which should be checked by more "controlled" observation
Minimal (e.g., binoculars)	Variables free to vary without control, but may be specifiable and their effect estimated	Good description of phenomena; knowledge of operating variables speculative, and "predictability" is therefore highly questionable	The observer must not be detected by what is being observed
Many diagnostic aids; precision relatively weak	Variables free to vary without control, but may be specifiable and their effect estimated	Good description of phenomena; knowledge of operating variables speculative, and "predictability" is therefore highly questionable	Stress is on the single case, and the major interest is applied
Many aids which make observing clearer	Variables free to vary, but *are* specifiable, and their effects can be estimated with reasonable accuracy	Probability of repeatability is reasonably high, but with considerable variation in degree of error in prediction	Statistical analysis leads to determination of the contribution of each variable
High-powered instruments of great precision	Variables so well known that the predictions of what will occur are confirmable	Precision only slightly less accurate, in general, than the laboratory experiment	Scientist limited by time since he can make observations only when nature can provide the conditions for observation
Maximal use of equipment; present tendency is toward complete automaticity to the point where laboratory men may only read a few dials and meters	Most completely available "control" devised by man or nature to date	Highest validity possible because "controlled" experimental findings are repeatable within very small degree of error	No experiment is ever 100 per cent "controlled," but this fact does not detract from the value of experimentation

effects between two or more variables which cannot be determined via the usual classical experiment. An example of an analysis of variance design would be that of determining the effect of such variables as heredity (strain

Independent variables → → → → - - - → Dependent variable

Fig. 5. The analysis of variance designs

differences), vitamin intake, and glandular function upon longevity in a particular animal form such as the mouse or the dog. It might be found, for example, that the dog's life span is significantly shortened if a certain vitamin is not included in his diet whereas the other variables have no effect on his longevity. A certain strain of mouse, on the other hand, might live significantly longer than any of the other mouse strains and because of interaction effects, which would have to be investigated further, this particular strain of mice might live even longer when thyroidectomized.

The factor analysis designs are concerned with identifying the component parts of relatively complex phenomena. There are no independent and dependent variables as such in these designs, since the basic purpose is not to relate dependent and independent variables, but rather, to identify those variables which are common to several measurements. Thus, a pictorial representation of the factor analysis design would look like Figure 6.

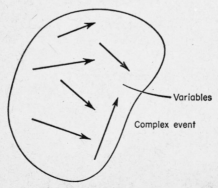

Variables

Complex event

Fig. 6. The factor analysis designs

If we let the oval shape represent a complex event such as pilot aptitude or the weather then the individual arrows within the oval shape represent the variables which are the components of pilot aptitude or the possible predictors of tomorrow's weather. The factorial approach can best be explained by an analogy. Many centuries ago early scientists described physical phenomena in terms of relatively gross units such as water and fire. Today the chemist does not speak of water, but rather of so much hydrogen and so much oxygen. In other words he has broken down a relatively complex phenomenon, water, into its component parts. Exactly the same step is taken in the factorial study of behavior. Let us take intelligence as an example. For the first few decades of modern psychology's existence the professional psychologist went along with the thinking of the man on the street concerning the nature of intelligence—namely, that if a person is smart, he is smart at everything, and if he is stupid, he is stupid at everything. This general intelligence concept is essentially what is behind the Binet, the Wechsler, and most of the early group varieties of intelligence tests. We come out with a single index of intelligence, the I.Q., which is supposed to tell us everything about man's intelligence.

Factor analysis has shown us that intelligence is not the unitary phenomenon most of us believed it to be, but rather, it is a complex, like water, which can be broken down into component parts. Some of the component parts of intelligence are Memory, Space, Reasoning, Perception, Number, Verbal Comprehension, and Verbal Fluency. Individuals differ in their particular profiles. Person A may be high in the Number, Space, and Reasoning components and relatively low in all the others, whereas person B may be just the reverse. In this connection, it should be noted that these two individuals could even have exactly the same I.Q., but the distribution of their high and low points would differ. This point is brought out graphically by the two profiles depicted in Figure 7. If we average each of these two profiles, we get exactly the same value, namely 50. This would be equivalent to an I.Q. of 100. If the I.Q. were the only information available, we would conclude that these two

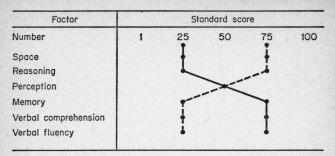

Factor	Standard score				
Number	1	25	50	75	100
Space					
Reasoning					
Perception					
Memory					
Verbal comprehension					
Verbal fluency					

Fig. 7. Standard scores of two persons, A (solid line) and B (dotted line), with the same I.Q. but with opposite mental-ability profiles

individuals are intellectually identical. It is obvious, however, that they are identical only in their performance on the perception factor. Otherwise person A is essentially quantitative in his intellectual strength, whereas person B is essentially verbal.

The theoretical and practical implications of this relatively new analytic approach are truly revolutionary, both for our understanding of human individuality and for the possibilities it is opening up for optimal utilization of human resources in terms of educational and vocational guidance. The implications of multiple-variable designs for the further advancement of science are even more revolutionary, and we have just begun to sound out their possibilities. They are truly 20th-century revolutions, for these developments are primarily due to the contemporary biologist R. A. Fisher[3] (analysis of variance, around 1915-1930) and to the recently deceased psychologist L. L. Thurstone[4] (multiple factor analysis, around 1930-1940). These conceptual-observational methods are revolutionary because they permit the scientist to observe many variables simultaneously under experimentally and statistically assessable "controlled" conditions. In other words, these experimental designs are peculiarly appropriate to multiple-variable domains such as the biological, psychological, and social sciences. And the controlled experiment, whether single variable or multi-variable in design, represents the most convincing procedure yet devised by man for identifying the "facts" of the various scientific disciplines.

ON SCIENTIFIC THEORY

The history of the development of each of the modern sciences from a philosophical realm of speculation to a theoretically integrated system of experimental facts has been surprisingly similar. The need for each field to conquer problems of measurement and problems of controlled observation is a very important part of this history. Perhaps we can briefly summarize this historical pattern by saying that all scientific inquiry is characterized by four successive stages: (a) pre-scientific philosophical speculation, (b) exploratory observation (empirical), (c) experimentation and quantification, and (d) mathematical rationalization and theoretical unification. Physics, for example, has passed through all four stages and stands as a model for the less mature sciences to follow. Biology appears to be somewhere just beyond the third phase, having achieved relatively little overall theoretical unification. Psychology has barely tapped the fourth phase of scientific development, and can be characterized today as being somewhere between phases two (empirical) and three (experimental). Thus, we see that an embryonic field such as psychology has not moved very far in the direction of theoretical unification; whereas a field such as physics is so highly rationalized as to require a thorough familiarity with mathematics in order to be able to navigate minimally within its framework. This brief historical overview also brings out the point that the scientific enterprise both begins and ends with theory. That is, it starts with the speculative query, and after taking on sufficient empirical armament, it attempts to wrap it all up in an orderly, rational bundle. This observation points up the fact that the rational aspect of science is, in effect, always with us, even though it may be somewhat submerged when a growing science passes through its adolescent empirical stages. After all, of what use are factual particulars, except as phenomenal "for instances" of a general principle?

Theory, then, represents the more rational side of

science, for it is concerned with supplying overarching structures on which the "facts" can hang their meaning. It might do this arranging facts or classifying them at a more or less descriptive level, as in the case of the Linnaeus biological taxonomy. Or, it might do this at a more explanatory level by subsuming facts under laws or hypotheses, brought within focus by a few generally unifying concepts and relationships, as in the case of Newton or Einstein. There is a very broad range of conceptualizing which goes on under the name of theory. It ranges all the way from giving a name to a new phenomenon to developing a unified theory of the universe.

Empiricism without conscious attempts at conceptualizing and showing logical relationships simply does not lead automatically to theoretical unification. The history of science is replete with instances where all the facts were in, but because of the lack of an interested and insightful theorist, the development of the unifying concept, law, or theory was retarded. Facts remain isolated until some synthesizing mind brings them together. Unfortunately, the concern for the practical and the observable, and the corresponding lack of concern for the theoretical, pervades our entire American culture and, to a considerable extent, the culture of Western civilization. It is generally agreed that scientific theorists have come out of European rather than American institutions of higher learning.[5] The revolutionary thinkers, such as Einstein, Darwin, and Freud, are outstanding examples of this point. American science, on the other hand, has been strong in the applied fields, technology of motor cars, military hardware, and clinical practice. I have no objection to America's strength in applied science. I am simply deploring our lack of similar concern for basic science and, in particular, within the framework of pure science, our lack of support for the theoretically oriented scientist.

One way of identifying what a nation values is by an analysis of how it spends its money. We all know that the American people do not have much faith in the egghead because they spend very little, proportionately, on intellectual matters. The proportion of the national

income which is spent on education and research is between 6 and 7 percent. Ninety-five percent of research
funds are devoted to the physical sciences, with the bulk
of that money being spent on such humanistic items as
atomic and hydrogen bombs and rockets. Most of the
remaining 5 percent is distributed among the biological
and medical sciences. A tiny fraction of the 5 percent is
available for the behavioral and social sciences. Most of
this research money is devoted to efforts which show a
fairly immediate practical payoff, and, of course, the assumption is that results will only pay off if we somehow
gather data. In spite of the fact that we know we cannot
have applied science unless we have basic science, we
do little to support basic science. In spite of the fact
that basic science requires integrating theory in order to
flourish, we do little to support basic theory. In spite
of our very real awareness that, in the long run, there
is actually nothing more practical than good theory, we
do little to support its development. We do all this even
though we know that Einstein's famous equation $E = mc^2$, written in 1905 by a man who spent his lifetime
working primarily with pencil, paper, and his *head*, is
the basis for modern physical theory and the practical
applications which are currently developing therefrom.

And why do we do all this? Because the contemporary
myth is that theoretical efforts are not sufficiently scientific. Such stuff smacks too much of the armchair, we
are told. It is not only the politicians in Washington who
think this way; in some cases it includes members of the
scientific fraternity who have been swamped by the modern empirical wave. The error which is committed in
this view is the usual straw-man error; no serious theoretical scientist is concerned about concepts, principles,
and laws unless they mesh with the observed facts. He
recognizes the attendant risks in theorizing, but he also
realizes that we do not have science without theory. In
fact, the psychologist E. G. Boring goes so far as to say
that:

Science is *theory*—descriptive theory sometimes, and explanatory theory at other times, yet theory, because it is con-

cerned with constructs that are things and their relations. Science [is] empirically based. You check constantly against phenomenal particulars but you are after the generalities that the particulars yield.[6]

Boring's comment brings out the key thought in understanding the scientific enterprise. Science is not "just the facts," nor is it theory divorced from fact. The genius of science lies in the stringent way in which it requires that the two mutually support each other. Such epistemic correlation[7] is provided for in Figure 1 by the dotted lines which connect various combinations of the four approaches to reality. The correlation of empiricism and rationalism of science, for example, is connected by line B. When we combine this demand with the criterion of empirical repeatability indicated in Figure 3, we see why the epistemologist feels relatively secure about what gets wrung out of the scientific methodological machinery.

LOGICAL POSITIVISM

Why and how did logical positivism come into being? What questions does it ask and who are its major proponents? It would seem reasonable to suggest that a particular philosophic position comes into being in the natural course of events, out of the problems and the tradition of a given culture. Thus, since the development of modern science at the time of the Renaissance, philosophers have paid more and more attention to advancements in science as the platform from which they have made their metaphysical leaps. This is evident in the Copernican revolution, which led to a heliocentric rather than a geocentric conception of the universe; in the impact of Darwin on the subsequent development of evolutionary theories of man, nature, and society; and in the influence of psychology on contemporary theorizing on unconscious processes and existentialism as they relate to various facets of man's nature.

This wedding of philosophy and science has become more and more self-conscious, so that among contemporary philosophers we now have a specialty known as philosophy of science. And within this specialty, there has emerged a group of philosophers who have revolted against the traditional philosophy of speculation and insist that this must be supplanted by a scientific philosophy —an approach to ultimate issues which is patterned after the highly fruitful epistemology and methodology of the scientific enterprise. The following quote from Reichenbach summarizes the essence of their revolt and affirmation:

> There is more error than truth in traditional philosophy. . . . The glorification of the philosophies of the past, the presentation of the various systems as so many versions of wisdom, each in its own right, has undermined the philosophic potency of the present generation. . . . Scientific philosophy . . . insists that the question of truth must be raised within philosophy in the same sense as in the sciences. . . . The new philosophy is itself empirical and is satisfied with empirical truth.[8]

Feigl [9] points out that there were three major developments in science which gave rise to logical positivism. Very briefly, these are the revolutionary studies of Bertrand Russell and Hilbert on the logical foundations of mathematics; the shaking of the conceptual foundations of physics by such thinkers as Einstein, Planck, Bohr, and Heisenberg; and the influence of behaviorism (Pavlov and Watson) on psychology. All of these developments, in addition to shaking up the erroneous tendency toward the absolutizing of knowledge, eventually pointed the finger at the problem of language and the business of trying to communicate meanings. The crusade for a more scientific philosophy found its leadership in Europe, particularly in Austria, among a small group of scientists and philosophers who have since come to be known as the Vienna Circle.[10] It is important to note that many of these men had training and experience as scientists before engaging in philosophy. In other words, they knew, from first-hand experience, something of the trials and tribulations of establishing a scientific finding.[11] And they were impressed with the validity of knowledge which emerged. Rudolf Carnap, for example, was a physicist for many years before he turned his thinking to the logical foundations of philosophical and scientific language. It would appear that these thinkers were primarily impressed with the testability of the scientist's statements, for they felt that the scientific approach could best answer what they regard as the most fundamental philosophical questions: What do you mean? and How do you know?

Let us pursue the question of meaning first. Reichenbach introduces us to this point quite potently in the very first paragraph of his book *The Rise of Scientific Philosophy* by quoting the following passage from a standard philosophical work: "Reason is substance, as well as infinite power, its own infinite material underlying all the natural and spiritual life; as also the infinite form, that which sets the material in motion. Reason is the substance from which all things derive their being." [12] The immediate response to this is that it is meaningless. The logical positivist wants to eliminate such verbal nonsense, which, unfortunately, has represented too much of the contributions of philosophy. One way in which their analysis of meaning and language has been helpful is the distinction they make between cognitive (factual) and non-cognitive (emotive) meaning. Cognitive meanings refer to those statements which are factual or logical in nature; such statements are purely informational or intellectual, devoid of affective intent, and are best conveyed via one form or another of neutral prose. Non-cognitive or affective meanings, on the other hand, are emotive or expressive in nature; such statements are meant to convey feeling, value, or intent, and are best conveyed via a more symbolic language such as poetry or the other art forms.

Up to this point I have no objection to the scientifically oriented philosopher. I think we can clearly say that he has had a most salutary effect on muddled philosophic thought and that, via his precise analysis of the structure and function of language, as exemplified by the clear-cut distinction between cognitive and non-cognitive meaning, he has actually succeeded in cutting away much of the verbal jungle[13] with which philosophy inevitably finds itself embroiled. It is when we move into the other question, How do you know? that I doubt the position of the logical positivist. At this point the logical positivist commits the "nothing but" or reductive error. He takes a good thing—namely, the scientist's way of knowing, his convincing criteria of testability—and insists that these criteria provide the *only* valid approach to knowledge. He does penetrating analyses of the formal or logical aspect of science and even creates new notations in the form of symbolic logic and metalanguages. On the other side of the scientific coin, the empirical, he performs equally brilliant analyses of the necessity for inter-subjectivity in reporting a sensory observation, analyses of the procedures for establishing an operational concept, and, in fact, has developed what some people have called a science of science.[14] All this is fine as an analysis of the scientific enterprise. And further, such analysis is needed for the advancement of science because the scientists themselves do not make sufficient analyses of their presuppositions. They are too swallowed up in the business of gathering data and generating hypotheses and theories to ask penetrating questions about whether or not they are going about their business properly. From this point of view they "know" that they are proceeding correctly, simply because they are very skillfully utilizing techniques which are essentially accepted by the scientific community. In short, it is much easier for the "outsider" philosopher of science than it is for the workaday scientist to make an objective analysis and assessment of the situation, climb up high in his ivory tower, and scream invectives at the busy scientific workers to change directions, tactics, or tools, in order to accomplish the task more adequately. In this regard the scientific community owes a vast amount to the small and hearty band of scientific philosophers. But when they make pronouncements such as "The meaning of a statement is determined by the way in which it can be verified, *where its being verified consists in its being tested by empirical observation*,[15] or, "The method of logical syntax, that is, analysis of the formal structure of language as a system of rules, is the *only* method of philosophy" [16] they fall into the trap which ensnares many a good systematist—namely, overextension of a point of view.

If we should go along with the logical positivist at this juncture, we should be forced to the conclusion that there is no cognitive meaning or truth to most of the arts, religion, and literature. We should have to conclude that such utterances are merely the affective expressions of

man in his irrational moments—the mere grunts and
groans of man in moments of ecstasy or tribulation. Careful analysis of the situation indicates that this interpretation simply will not hold up. It is true that the advances
in the sciences have tended to eclipse the knowledge-
giving qualities of non-scientific disciplines. And it is also
true that the verifiability criteria in the humanistic domains are fuzzy in contrast to those in science, but it
does *not* follow from this that such lines of pursuit are
devoid of knowledge. F. S. C. Northrop, in the *Logic of
the Sciences and the Humanities*,[17] points out that the
humanistic disciplines simply cannot be adequately understood in terms of the usual scientific criteria. He points
to the greater involvement of intuition in such endeavors,
which he refers to as "immediate aesthetic awareness."
Carver[18] points to the need for training in aesthetic
awareness as a prerequisite for a meaningful encounter
in the arts. He speaks of this awareness as "sensitivity"
and insists that if one comes to the artistic product
sufficiently talented and prepared, it is at least as "meaningful" as the cognitive meaning of the logical positivist.
"The point is that assertions about the structure of works
of art are matters of belief based on evidence open to
observation but only to competent observers. The necessity for competence puts a limit on the intersubjec-
tivity of the procedures which verify these statements
about the structure of works of art." [19] And later, reflecting on the understanding of a poem, he points out
that it is "perceivable only by the sufficiently sensitive
observer, to whom alone will statements about the structural elements of poetry be meaningful but to whom
such statements will be as meaningful as statements
about the height of his grandmother."

Carver's views are potent, and germane to the argu-
ments of the logical positivists, because he has chosen
to deal with them on their own ground. That is, Carver's
monograph is an explicit and self-conscious attempt to
analyze the question of cognitive meaning from *within*
the framework of logical positivism. This can be seen
merely from the sub-title of his essay, *The Application
to Aesthetics of the Logical Positivist's Verifiability Criteria of Cognitive Meaning*. The point is that he is able

to demonstrate the presence of cognitive meaning in art, a position which is contrary to the views of the logical positivists. The radical positivist sees humanistic disciplines as conveyng non-cognitive or emotive meanings only, whereas the proponents of these disciplines see the presence of both cognitive and non-cognitive meanings in their works.

Perhaps Carver points to the crux of the difficulty when he says, "If one is attempting to form a translatability criterion of cognitive meaning with universal application, he must not formulate it in terms of a language of science, or a language of esthetics, but rather must formulate it in terms of a language more basic than either and including both as component parts." [20] Some recent contributions to philosophic thought may constitute the answer to Carver's challenge. I am thinking of such works as Ernst Cassirer's three volumes on *The Philosophy of Symbolic Forms*, and Suzanne Langer's two volumes, *Philosophy in a New Key* and *Feeling and Form*. These efforts constitute a philosophy of symbolic forms, in which the major cultural achievements, religion, language, art, literature, philosophy, and science, are viewed as manifestations of man's conceptual and creative capabilities. In short, all of these expressions are seen as meaningful, symbolic forms. The suggestion is that we look to these forms for what they can convey to us, that is, that we analyze them in a way which is consistent with the nature of the form, and that we do *not* commit the reductive error, and insist that one set of criteria be applied to all kinds of symbolic expression. Langer makes this point the title[21] of one of her books, and says, in effect, that its full realization will reconstruct philosophy "in a new key."

> In the fundamental notion of symbolization—mystical, practical, or mathematical, it makes no difference—we have the keynote of all humanistic problems. In it lies a new conception of "mentality" that may illumine questions of life and consciousness, instead of obscuring them as traditional "scientific methods" have done. If it is indeed a generative idea, it will beget tangible methods of its own. . . . The philosophical study of symbols . . . has arisen in the fields that the great advance of learning has left fallow. Perhaps it

holds the seed of a new intellectual harvest, to be reaped in the next season of the human understanding.[22]

Furthermore, there is good reason to believe that the scientific enterprise is enmeshed in more metaphysics than the logical positivists will admit to. They are so busy justifiably opposing non-testable concepts that they seem to have overlooked what ought to be obvious to them—namely, the inescapability of metaphysical involvement when taking any philosophical position, including the position of "no position" or the position of logical positivism. On this particular issue, we find science in the peculiar position of being unwilling to say that it is as metaphysically pure as certain philosophers say it is. One example of the inextricable intermeshing of science and metaphysics is given by Cornelius Lanczos, a European theoretical physicist, in a recent article on Einstein and the role of theory in contemporary physics.

> What Einstein did was not a formal accomplishment. He did not approach the problem from the standpoint of finding some mathematical equation which will describe a certain group of phenomena. Something much more fundamental was at stake, namely, *the critical evaluation of the cultural foundation of theoretical physics.* [Italics mine—J.R.R.] Certain things which were always taken for granted, were put under scrutiny and their falseness proved. This was no longer mere physics and mathematics. . . . Here started that dogged uphill fight of Einstein which lasted for 10 years and which is perhaps unparalleled in the entire history of the human mind: a fight which did not arise from any experimental puzzle but from a purely philosophical puzzle of the mind.[23]

This metaphysical foundation which underlies the assumptions of any scientist is insightfully expounded in the physicist-philosopher Margenau's book *The Nature of Physical Reality.* He elaborates, for example, the following six metaphysical requirements for good theory in science: (1) Constructs must possess logical fertility. (2) Constructs must have multiple connections. (3) Theory must have permanence and stability. (4) Extensibility of constructs. (5) The requirement of causality and (6) The requirement of simplicity and elegance.

His answer to the question, Where do metaphysical guiding principles come from? is: "They first emerge in the stream of experience as tentative expedients, grow into implicit beliefs with increasing application, and finally, strengthened by repeated success, pervade the entire texture of our theories about the world." [24]

What we have here, then, is the suggestion that we not be taken in by the literalistic epistemological position of the positivist; that we, instead, take a new look at the problem of knowledge. When we do this we come up with the idea of symbolic knowledge,[25] the idea that symbols convey meanings, and that different kinds of symbols are to be analyzed and understood according to the disciplinary context from which they emerge. I am urging that we not be blinded by the dazzling light of scientific progress by insisting that scientific ways of knowing are the *only* valid ways to truth. In short, I am saying that the position of radical logical positivism leads to encapsulation just as readily as do any number of other approaches to reality, in spite of its justifiable claim to truth. I am saying that logical positivism is probably the most potent epistemological approach available to man, but I am also saying that it cannot claim to be the *only* approach to truth. It cannot win the argument of truth by definition—that is, by simply stating that we will accept as true only those propositions which meet positivistic criteria. For in so doing, this position simply leaves out too much and emasculates itself.

Herbert Feigl is an excellent spokesman for what I call unencapsulated logical positivism, for he sees the value of it in total perspective. He says on the one hand that "Intuitive metaphysics, convinced of the existence of a privileged shortcut to 'truth,' mistakes having an experience for knowing something about it." On the other hand, he points out that ". . . the positivistic critique of metaphysics is primarily an attack upon confusion of meanings and is not intended as a wholesale repudiation of what has been presented under that label." Later, relating this point to the field of psychology, he points out that "If some of the extremely tough-minded psychologists relegate questions such as those concerning the instincts, the unconscious, or the relative roles of

constitution and environment to the limbo of metaphysics, then they cut with Ockham's razor far into the
flesh of knowledge instead of merely shaving away the
metaphysical whiskers." [26] The reference to psychology
reminds us of John B. Watson, who, in an earlier day,
was given to such ridiculous positions as consciously deny-
ing his own consciousness. The exclusion of classes of
data or of other approaches as legitimate knowledge on
the grounds that it does not fit one's presuppositions has
repeatedly led us down blind alleys rather than along the
royal road to truth.

NOTES

1. The reader might well ask why the writer has made
science and logical positivism his special target. My answer is
based on the present apparent impregnability of science. Science
looks relatively infallible, scientists appear to be demi-gods,
and the scientific world-view is the 20th-century myth. (See,
for example, A. Standen, *Science is a Sacred Cow*, New York:
E. P. Dutton & Co., 1950.) If it can be demonstrated that even
our most highly honored approach to reality, science, is subject
to encapsulation, then it follows that all other approaches are
at least suspect. Thus, my view is that scholars in the humanities are equally encapsulated in their approach to reality. While
he is primarily concerned with bridging the two cultures of
science and the humanities, the British novelist-scientist C. P.
Snow offers a critique (see *The Two Cultures and the Scientific
Revolution*, New York: Cambridge University Press, 1959)
which has implications for the encapsulation of experts in the
humanities. He says, for example, "They are impoverished too
—perhaps more seriously, because they are vainer about it.
They still like to pretend that the traditional culture is the
whole of 'culture,' as though the natural order didn't exist.
. . . Yet most non-scientists have no conception of that edifice
at all. Even if they want to have it, they can't. It is rather as
though, over an immense range of intellectual experience, a
whole group was tone-deaf. Except that this tone-deafness
doesn't come by nature, but by training, or rather the absence
of training" (pp. 13-14). A similar analysis is offered by the
chemist H. G. Cassidy, *The Sciences and the Arts*, New York:
Harper and Bros., 1962.
2. See A. Koyre, *From the Closed World to the Infinite
Universe*, New York: Harper & Bros., 1957.
3. R. A. Fisher, *The Design of Experiments*, London:

Oliver & Boyd, 4th Edition, 1947. For something more readable see an elementary statistical text such as H. E. Garrett, *Statistics for Students of Psychology and Education*, New York: Longmans, Green & Co., 1959.

4. L. L. Thurstone, *Multiple Factor Analysis*, Chicago: The University of Chicago Press, 1947. The most readable of the half dozen or so books on this subject is B. Fruchter, *Introduction To Factor Analysis*, Princeton: D. Van Nostrand Company, Inc., 1954.

5. Of course, there are exceptions. These might include the theoretical geneticist T. H. Morgan, the physical chemist Willard Gibbs, and possibly the psychologist-philosopher William James.

6. E. G. Boring, The role of theory in experimental psychology, *American Journal of Psychology*, 1953, 66, 169-184.

7. This is a concept of the philosopher Northrop. See F. S. C. Northrop, *The Logic of the Sciences and the Humanities*, New Haven: Yale University Press, 1947.

8. H. Reichenbach, *The Rise of Scientific Philosophy*, Berkeley: University of California Press, 1951, pp. 325-326.

9. H. Feigl, Logical Empiricism. In D. H. Runes, *Twentieth Century Philosophy*, New York: Philosophical Library, 1943, pp. 371-417.

10. The Vienna Circle included the following: Rudolf Carnap, Herbert Feigl, Phillip Frank, Kurt Godel, Hans Hahn, Felix Kaufmann, Victor Kraft, Otto Neurath, Moritz Schlick, and Friedrich Waisman. In addition to this inner group of scholars who met regularly in Vienna in the twenties, there were other associates who were more or less remote either in terms of distance, time, or opinion. These included A. J. Ayer, Carl Hempel, Joergen Joergensen, Karl Menger, Charles W. Morris, Karl Popper, Hans Reichenbach, and Richard von Mises. See J. O. Urmson, *Western Philosophy and Philosophers*, New York: Hawthorn Books, Inc., 1960, p. 240.

11. My colleague, and one of my critical readers, Ludwig von Bertalanffy, makes the point, however, that *none* of these men has made a significant contribution to the advancement of science *per se*. One implication of this, he feels, is that the positivists seem to be commentators on science rather than makers of science. In other words, the fact that the logical positivists have not been sufficiently involved in the first-hand creation of science has served as a detriment to their understanding of science.

12. H. Reichenbach, *op. cit.*, p.e.

13. Professor Hunnex suggests that the logical positivist is embroiled in a verbal jungle of his own concerning the exact nature of the verifiability principle of meaning.

14. See S. S. Stevens, The science of science, *Psychological Bulletin*, 1939, 36, 221-263; C. W. Morris, *Sign, Language and Behavior*, New York: Prentice-Hall, 1946; and P. Bridgman, *The Logic of Modern Physics*, New York: Macmillan, 1928.

15. A. J. Ayer, *The Revolution in Philosophy*, London: St. Martin's Press, 1956, p. 74.

16. R. Carnap, *Meaning and Necessity*, Chicago: University of Chicago Press, 1947.

17. F. S. C. Northrop, *op. cit.*

18. G. A. Carver, *Aesthetics and the Problem of Meaning*, New Haven: Yale University Press, 1952.

19. *Ibid.*, p. 59.

20. *Ibid.*, p. 74.

21. Suzanne Langer, *Philosophy in a New Key*, Cambridge: Harvard University Press, 1942.

22. *Ibid.*, pp. 19-20.

23. Cornelius Lanczos, Einstein and the role of theory in contemporary physics, *American Scientist*, 1959, 47, 41-59.

24. Henry Margenau, *The Nature of Physical Reality*, New York: McGraw-Hill, 1950, p. 81. Donald T. Campbell provides us with an excellent social psychological and philosophical analysis of Margenau's position in his recent article under the title "Blind variation and selective thought as in other knowledge processes," *Psychol. Review*, 1960, 67, 380-400. In short, Campbell makes the point that all advances in knowledge involve a process of blind variation and selective retention. Trial and error, then, followed by retention of those breakthroughs which lead to pay dirt, is the answer offered by Margenau and Campbell on the origin of guiding principles of scientific theory construction.

25. This concept, along with the works of Cassirer and Langer, is discussed at greater length in Chapter 8.

26. H. Feigl, *op. cit.*, pp. 384, 385, and 387.

5

The Problem of Meaninglessness

*"And the wind shall say: 'Here were decent godless people
Their only monument the asphalt road
And a thousand lost golf balls.'"*

—T. S. Eliot

*"The tragedy of our age is the awful incommunicability of
souls."*

—W. O. Martin

Thus far we have seen that man's search for reality
has led him to multiple visions of truth. Instead of a
royal road to truth he has had to move along the craggy
road of relativism. Even his most certain pathway to
knowledge, that of science and logical positivism, cannot
come to grips with ultimate reality. Thus, we have seen
that specialists err when they pronounce ultimate truth
from the perspective of a limited reality image. The scientist sees things through the literal glasses of the logical
positivist, the artist sees things through the depth symbol
of the intuitionist, and the mathematician sees things in
terms of logical abstractions. In short, they are encapsulated. Thus, we conclude that finite man cannot know
ultimate reality, which is infinite, and that what man has
variously called ultimate reality throughout the pages
of recorded history represents projections of "reality images" across the epistemological barrier into the unattain-
able realm of the ultimate. The claim of absolute truth
turns out, upon close analysis, to reduce to relative truth.
The fact that we are forced to several "reality images"
rather than converging on one is regarded by many thinkers as the essence of the problem of "meaning."

THE RELATIVITY OF VALUES

Man, of course, has always had to come to grips with
the meaning of things, but why does the problem of

"meaninglessness" seem to be the peculiarly central problem of 20th-century man? No doubt the uncertainty of man's continuance due to the production of atomic and hydrogen bombs, other rapid scientific and technological advancements, and similar revolutionary changes on the contemporary social and political scene have forced 20th-century man to be more introspective about his nature, but underneath the flow of external events lurks the question of human values and the "inner man." Modern thought seems clear on the point that no life can be whole unless it is meaningful and that meaning is clearly tied to the problem of values. In the past our perceptions of reality and our notions of value were not as shakily relative as they seem to be today. Traditional views of reality and value seemed more permanent and stable, and it was easier to live meaningfully in such an ethos than it is to live in the fluid ethos of the 20th century. For example, during the Middle Ages reality was defined, and very clearly, by the priests of the church. There was certainty about the nature of reality, and the process of living in accordance with such stability was secure and relatively simple. After the doubts and re-evaluation of the Renaissance, a new, but even more secure (so we were told), approach to reality came upon the scene in the guise of modern science. Science had the great advantage of providing very tangible results, both in the form of a clearly statable machinery for differentiating between knowledge and not-knowledge, and in the sense of technological products such as steamboats, telephones, refrigerators, and television. Scientists were convinced they knew how to get the answers, and the future of man and "progress" were just a matter of grinding things out via the scientific method. The 19th century and early 20th century mechanistic view of the universe left little for the physical scientist to do but compute the next decimal point. Then came such things as Einstein's theory of relativity, the Heisenberg indeterminacy principle, the admission of the unpredictability of the single case, the emergence of non-mechanistic concepts such as dynamic fields, organizers, and *Gestalts*, and finally, of course, atomic energy. The result was that the completely materialistic view of things and the inevitable forward movement of mankind no longer appeared to be so secure or so obvious. The main point to be made here is that neither the priority of values provided by the medieval church nor those provided by 19th-century science seem to have guaranteed man anything about the nature of reality or the meaningfulness of life.

The lack of an absolute standard of truth has led to a lack of an absolute value, which in turn leaves man embroiled in the ambiguity from which he has been hoping to escape in his quest for the ultimately real. The lack of a single truth around which to order one's life is distressing to most people. This assertion receives a more complete analysis in Chapters 6 and 7, but perahps it would be in order to comment briefly on this point now, particularly as it relates to the complex interplay between knowledge and value. The distress which accompanies the realization of relative rather than absolute truth is inevitable because it forces the individual to break out of his presently encapsulated world view and to reconstruct another world picture out of the remaining chaos. The full awareness that no one approach to reality can be counted upon for thoroughly stable results means that its value as a guide for meaningful living is somewhat reduced. At the same time other approaches to reality now become more meaningful, but similarly, no one approach can maintain itself absolutely because of its inherent limitations. Psychologically, each approach to reality is differentially reinforced, which means that different approaches to reality take on different values for a given individual. The result is an individual psycho-epistemological hierarchy, a hierarchy which gives the highest value to that truth criterion which leads to the greatest sense of personal meaning. Within the limits of his psychobiological equipment, it is obvious that considerable choice is involved in the evolution of a value hierarchy. But the freedom to choose one's values is too big a choice for the average man, and he tends to drift and to oscillate in the face of a multi-valued universe. The writings of the existentialists and of social psychologists and psychoanalysts such as David Riesman[1] and Erich Fromm[2] even go so far as to suggest that *man does not want the freedom to choose his values!* Riesman's other-directed man would prefer to follow the herd rather than follow the dictates of his underlying individuality, not because he believes in the herd, but because there is a greater consequent feeling of security (i.e., less ambiguity). Fromm takes this analysis many steps further and points out that modern man prefers to be told what to do by strong, authoritarian leaders, that he wants his values in an absolute form, handed down to him, that a Hitler is a very understandable and perhaps unconsciously desired product of our times, and that we literally want to escape from freedom. In a similar vein, a favorite theme of the existentialists is the "terror" of freedom. Sartre[3] states that man is free to choose, and further, that he and he alone is responsible for his choice. No blaming things on God, mother, or country. Man chooses his values, and he makes himself.[4] This is a very realistic subjectivism, and, in my estimation, one needs strong shoulders to play the existentialist game. The existentialist "failures" in Sartre's literary products such as *No Exit* and *The Flies*[5] are potent examples. The fact that so many readers see only despair and meaninglessness in the works of modern existentialism is also a sign of the times. As I see it, these miserable creatures of Sartre's represent the struggle of modern man in trying to come to grips with the problem of meaning. The fact that they so often end up in despair is simply a statement about the condition of modern man. And the fact that so many readers of Sartre see despair, and no hope, is a further reflection of the meaningless perceptual framework of 20th-century man. In one of his poems, T. S. Eliot says we are "hollow men," [6] and in *The Cocktail Party* he explores the "empty" ramifications of 20th-century godlessness. Celia, in her dialogue with Reilly, sums it up in these three lines:

> It's not the feeling of anything I've done,
> Which I might get away from, or of anything in me
> I could get rid of—but of emptiness.[7]

THOUGHT CONTROL

Huxley[8] and Orwell [9] move from meaninglessness, hollowness, and emptiness to thingness or "mechanical" man. That is, they take highly specialized, industrialized, robotized, automatized, non-feeling, non-thinking man as we know him in our highly industrialized Western civilization, and they fictitiously take this dehumanization process to its logical conclusion. One of their major themes is that individuality gets crushed by the state. Unfortunately, it is not necessary to turn to fiction to realize the truth of this prediction. We merely have to recount the recent totalitarianisms of the fascists, the nazis, and other forms of dictatorship. Even democratic socialism runs the risk of losing the individual in one of the closets of bureaucracy. Bureaucrats in a democratic world, of course, recognize the political equality of the individual, but many Britishers are of the opinion that the humanness of a person, both of the bureaucrat and of the member of socialist society who is being "serviced," somehow gets lost in the red tape.

Another conclusion of contemporary nihilistic literature is to the effect that "big brother" is not only watching, he is breathing down our backs! Vance Packard's *Hidden Persuaders* elucidates just how subtle "big brother" can be. The "hidden persuaders" are the advertising men of Madison Avenue, and they are apparently manipulating our minds more than we know. Let me take space to elaborate on only one of their more subtle techniques, an application of a well known experimental finding in the psychology laboratory. It is called subliminal advertising[10] and it is a modification of subliminal conditioning. In this particular brand of advertising "your friendly corner car-dealers" influence your mind at a subconscious level. They pepper you with propaganda to buy their product without your being aware of the fact that they are doing it. It is like learning something while you are asleep, or like being propagandized while under hypnosis. In other words, short of turning off your television set, you have no control over what they feed into your brain!

Pavlov was the first man to describe the conditioned response, a response which occurs when a new stimulus elicits an old and well established reaction. In the situation of the classical dog experiment Pavlov paired a bell stimulus with a food stimulus. The old stimulus might be the placing of a piece of meat in the mouth of a

dog. The normal response to this is salivation, as part of
the usual digestive process.[11] But if we repeatedly associate bell with meat, for let us say 100 to 200 trials, it
will then be possible to present the bell stimulus alone
and elicit the salivary response. Thus, the sound of a
bell, which previously had absolutely no connection with
salivation, is now capable of initiating the salivary response. It has since been demonstrated that an organism,
including man, under the proper circumstances, can be
"conditioned" to any stimulus which he is capable of
"receiving." And so men have "learned" to like women
named Helen, or soups named Campbell, or cars named
Ford, or to hate women named Helen, or the color green,
or what have you. The situation gets quite complicated
in terms of such phenomena as reinforcement, generalization, differentiation, higher-order conditioning, experimental extinction, and spontaneous recovery. There are
mountains of experimental findings on conditioning, and,
as is generally known, much of our behavior can be accounted for on the basis of these findings. Subliminal
conditioning, that is, establishing a conditioned response
in an organism in an unconscious state, is one of the more
recent investigations of the conditioned response. The
word "subliminal" literally means "below the limen," or
below the level of awareness. This experiment was conducted most convincingly on humans who were under
anesthesia. Many conditioning trials were given to an
anesthetized individual who was later presented with
the conditioned stimulus alone. Under the later condition, that is, the condition of no anesthesia, the subject
elicited a very clear conditioned response. This is the
principle which our hidden persuaders are exploiting.

There is nothing mysterious about all this, and there
is nothing phony about it, just as there is nothing phony
about the most recent step modern man has taken in
the direction of thought control—brainwashing. Brainwashing involves both physical fatigue and psychological
fatigue. And, as is well known from the psychological
literature on experimental neurosis, every man has his
breaking point in response to stress. Going back to Pavlov,
in the process of conditioning a dog to respond when
presented with a circle stimulus, Pavlov made the "dis-

crimination" task more and more difficult. That is, on
subsequent trials he made the circle more and more like
an ellipse, and the ellipse more and more like a circle.
When the discrimination task became too difficult the
animal's adaptive capacities broke down completely and
he became "neurotic." This was the first case of experimental neurosis, and it has been demonstrated repeatedly
on many animal forms. Similar research on "frustration
tolerance" has been conducted on human subjects. One
of the conclusions to be drawn from this research is that
in the face of a no-solution situation the subject will
pick at straws in order to adapt to his environment, and
when you remove the straws, the organism will break
down. It is nonsense to speak of cowardice when you
refer to a man who has been thoroughly "brainwashed."
It is not cowardice, but a fiendish application of the
psychology of conditioning and frustration. It is an example of one of the ways that a scientific finding can be
used for evil as well as for good, just as one can use
atomic energy for the purpose of blowing human kind
off the surface of the earth, as well as to provide a source
of energy for peaceful purposes. And it is an example of
thought control—the business of willfully and calcu-
latingly substituting one ideology for another.

MEANINGLESSNESS AND PHILOSOPHIC AWARENESS

The subject of brainwashing and thought control also
places the problems of encapsulation, epistemological
relativism, and value relativism into juxtaposition and
throws the consequent meaninglessness into high relief.
We cannot escape our childhood conditioning, and we
cannot escape the consequences of narrow, specialist
training and education. In other words, we can escape
encapsulation only to the extent that we educate away
from it. The fact that ideologies can be so readily planted
in and removed from the brains of men gives us good
reason to pause and ponder. How relative can our values
get! Imagine how meaningless one's existence can become
if "the powers that be" get full control of the brains of
men! We have pointed to some of the many signs that
individual men are losing their awareness and desire to

control their values, that they are willing for more willful men to "control" them in subtle and not-so-subtle ways. If the day comes when individual men lose control over which ideologies are permitted to enter their own brains and the brains of their sons and daughters, the time for men will cease, and the animals will take over. No man will have the "terror" of freedom, or the freedom of becoming his "self," or the problem of working out his reality image. He will have found what will appear to him as an "absolute" without even having to think about it!

The "emptiness" of contemporary man, and his inability to overcome his consequent perception of the absurdities of life and what the existentialists call the "anguish of being," is manifest in his daily life by his ultra-conforming behavior, his willingness to accept "positive thinking" rather than "ultimate concern" in the area of religion, and the eagerness with which he will pop tranquilizers into his mouth, shoot heroin into his arm, or develop alcoholism. Perhaps the most telling indication of the meaninglessness of modern man's existence is reflected in the rapid growth of psychology and psychiatry in this century. This is the age of psychology more because of our need to understand ourselves than because of what we know about human behavior or because we are an enlightened people. The dehumanization process suggests that man is dying, and the presence of "the bomb" suggests that man's "nothingness" may be closer than the existentialists think. About all that remains of humanity is an outer shell, for the "inner man" is on his last legs. And the 20th-century neurosis is the neurosis of purposelessness, meaninglessness, valuelessness, hollowness, or emptiness. No amount of tranquilizer drugs or "positive thinking" can cope with a situation of this magnitude. The depth probing of the psychotherapist or the meditative life of the reflective man is necessary here in order to help man come to grips with his "reality image." Like Sartre's existentialist failures, the contemporary neurotic gives up in despair in the face of freedom and responsibility to choose. The weight of the world descends upon the person with such a view, and the neurotic, under this kind of stress, simply sinks under the impact of "nothingness." Apparently what is devastating is the realization that "nothingness" does, in fact, exist as a legitimate choice, and the contemporary neurotic or existentialist failure seems drawn to such a choice by default. The "reality image" of the neurotic then, is constricted, distorted, and, of course, most confusing and difficult to live by. The kind of encapsulation we get in this case is one of impoverishment; the neurotic is not even convinced that there is enough in such an image to make the effort of existence worthwhile. Modern man seems to be saying something like this: If you can't convince me that there is some kind of ultimate reality, or if you can't convince me that there are certain absolute values by which I can live my life, I'll commit psychological suicide. That is, either convince me that there is "one truth" or one right way of doing things, or I'll conclude that everything is meaningless and I won't try any more.

The beatnik is an interesting case in point. While he is overwhelmed by a sense of meaninglessness, he is at least rebelling against being completely encapsulated. While it is true that his rebellion is not at the high level of philosophic disputation or international diplomacy, it does seem to represent a true rebuttal of contemporary values. The American beatnik is breaking with the "square," the 9 to 5 organization man. If nothing else he is at least determined to burst out of the capsule of tribal conditioning. In many ways it is an abortive effort, but it is a reflection of the spiritual sickness of the time. For, while these people do not know what it is they want, they at least know what they do not want—the contemporary, standard, phony American way of life. In short, they find it impossible to find "the existentially real" by conforming to the usual pattern of life. And so they take the step of complete non-conformism. The unfortunate aspect of the beatnik's situation is that the first step is the only step he takes. He does not go beyond this valid initial step to further valid steps. He merely steps out of character and remains "out."

My own personal reaction after having sat among the beatniks in North Beach, San Francisco, in Los Angeles, and in Greenwich Village is that they are psychologically very similar to what are known as social psychopaths, or, in more common parlance, bums. The social psychopath is a person who fails to adjust to society; he lives outside of society. He may reject the usual norms consciously or unconsciously, but he clearly rejects them. The juvenile delinquent, the professional hobo, and the criminal are all social psychopaths of varying degree. The beatnik has the same oppositions to society as the social psychopath, but, in general, he avoids the violent anti-societal acts of the thief and the thug. If the beatnik is a type of social bum, he is pretty high class, for he strikes me as reasonably intelligent, though highly undisciplined and spotty in his knowledge. Perhaps it might not be incorrect to characterize the beatniks as intellectual bums who have formed a very loosely organized club, or association of kindred travellers, going down the road of life looking rather pitifully and ineptly for a more meaningful mode of existence.

I get the impression that the "angry young men" at least have some guts left. The beatnik, you see, really is "beat," and wailing is about all he can do. He is disillusioned, and he's had it. The "angry young man," on the other hand, while disillusioned, is at least ready to stand up and fight for a better way of life—in short, he's not beat.[12] John Osborne and Colin Wilson are perhaps the best-known representatives of Britain's "angry young men." These young men are angry with their complacent and non-authentic elders. They are not willing to make believe they like what they see in contemporary political, social, and religious life. They see old symbols, such as those of royalty and of Christianity, as dead symbols, symbols which no longer carry meaning. It is not, as Colin Wilson says, that they do not want to believe, but rather, that they see through the non-living traditional symbols, and further, having seen through them, they are too honest to pretend they can believe in them. Wilson is particularly vocal on this point as it relates to the religious sphere. He clearly sees contemporary civilization in decline, and he offers *The Outsider*[13] as the heroic figure of our time. The contemporary Outsider, product of 20th-century fragmented life, has an acute need for meaning and purpose, for a driving sense of values. In short, the Outsider is today's truly religious man, our only hope for the salvation of a sick culture which will decline unless it recaptures religion at its core. The Outsider refuses to be sucked in by worldly values and abstract philosophies, but seeks instead that intensification and vitalizing involvement which gives life greater meaning. Osborne, of course, speaks his piece best in his plays. In *Look Back in Anger*[14] his characters mostly wail, and in this one they look more like beatniks. In *The Entertainer*[15] we continue to see people who are defeated by the meaninglessness of life, as in the case of Frank, but there are those who climb over the wailing wall, and either go down making a strong bid for nobility in life, as in the case of Archie Rice, who courageously faces the void, or they refuse to accept a false substitute, as in the case of the young girl, Jean. Osborne's and Wilson's concern for authenticity takes the form of real involvement as opposed to the neutralism or defeatism of the beatniks and the fakery of the "square" or the super-conformist. Osborne, for example, speaking about his lower-class parents and relatives, says, "They talked about their troubles in a way that would embarrass any middle-class observer. I've no doubt that they were often boring, but still *life had meaning for them.* Even if they did get drunk and fight, *they were responding; they were not defeated.*" [16]

The loss of meaning in traditional symbols has led to despair over the fact that absolutes do not exist, or if they do, that we do not seem to know how to make certain contact with them so that they can order our lives. With the angry young men, I suggest that we accept whatever 20th-century insights we have into our awareness and push on like men instead of mice. Why not face all truths squarely, that is, continue to be rigorous and disciplined about admitting potential candidates into the house of truth, but, once admitted, accept all items present and explain them for what they can mean to us rather than conclude that truth is simply too much to bear. The point is that the meaninglessness of modern man could be viewed as a sign of philosophic depth—a new awareness of the tragic side of life. The demand for honesty, even at the risk of destroying one's cherished beliefs, is surely indicative of philosophic maturity, an important step in the direction of "learning how to die." For as the old position is cast aside, a part of one's self does, in fact, die. But the implication of Montaigne's phrase, "to learn to philosophize is to learn how to die," is that the dying is necessary and desirable for it leads to a growing awareness of the totality of life. The meaninglessness of 20th-century man could represent more of an heroic quality than we have heretofore recognized. After all, it is not easy to look epistemological and value relativism squarely in the face and refuse to pick a value as our absolute for the sake of convenience or for the "peace of mind" it has to offer. It may well be that modern man has taken the first step toward becoming a visionary with respect to humanity. For as Colin Wilson points out, the Outsider ". . . does not prefer not to believe; he doesn't like feeling that futility gets the last word in the universe; his human nature would like to find something it can answer to with complete assent. But this honesty prevents his accepting a solution that he cannot reason about." [17]

In other words, the hope in the meaninglessness of contemporary man is this: If the truth is that there is no *single, ultimate* truth, or that we have no way of being certain about *the truth*, let us at least continually question whatever truth seems impregnable at a given point in time and space and accept meaninglessness if necessary, but let us also make the effort to move beyond the legitimate realities of the void. But in the process of doing this, let us not be deluded into the belief that one's personal "reality image" and its consequent meaning, is in fact, ultimate reality.

NOTES

1. David Riesman, *The Lonely Crowd*, New Haven: Yale University Press, 1950.

2. Erich Fromm, *Escape From Freedom*, New York: Ferrar and Rinehart, 1941.

3. Jean-Paul Sartre, *On Being and Nothingness*, New York: Philosophical Library, 1956.

4. See the discussion of values as it relates to free will versus determinism in Chapter 7.

5. Jean-Paul Sartre, *No Exit* and *The Flies*, New York: A. A. Knopf, 1947.

6. T. S. Eliot, *The Collected Poems and Plays*, "The Hollow Men," New York: Harcourt, Brace & World, Inc., 1936.

7. *Ibid.*, *The Cocktail Party*, p. 362.

8. Aldous Huxley, *Brave New World*, New York: Doubleday, Doran and Co., 1932.

9. George Orwell, *1984*, New York: Harcourt, Brace and Co., 1949.

10. The writer recognizes the fact that the claims regarding the *effectiveness* of subliminal advertising go beyond the facts. This point does not, however, detract from either the force or the intent of the argument as here presented. Nor does it cast doubt on the non-applied experimental work on subliminal conditioning which underlies subliminal advertising.

11. Pavlov was actually making a study of digestion, for which he won the Nobel Prize. His discovery of the conditioned response was quite accidental. It came about when he noticed that his dogs would salivate before he was able to put food in their mouths. In other words, it slowly dawned on him that he, Pavlov, was the conditioned stimulus for eliciting the conditioned response.

12. For a sampling of the literary efforts of both groups see Gene Feldman and Max Gartenberg, *The Beat Generation and The Angry Young Men*, New York: The Citadel Press, 1958.

13. Colin Wilson, *The Outsider*, New York: Houghton Mifflin Co., 1956. See also Wilson's *Religion and the Rebel*, London: Gollancz, 1957.

14. J. R. Osborne, *Look Back in Anger*, New York: Bantam Books, 1960.

15. J. R. Osborne, *The Entertainer*, New York: Bantam Books, 1960.

16. J. R. Osborne, They call it cricket, in *Declaration*, Colin Wilson (Ed.), London: MacGibbon & Kee Ltd., New York: E. P. Dutton Co., 1958, p. 64.

17. Colin Wilson, *op. cit.*, p. 120.

Part II

The Way Out?

"In the long run men give their supreme loyalties to over-all patterns of life, to those ideas and attitudes concerning the nature of the world and of life, which provide them with incentive and direction for living. These patterns of thought and action commonly have gone by the name of religion. Their importance is evidenced by the fact that no human society of any size is long without them, and by the fact that they outlive nations and governments."

—ARTHUR E. MORGAN

"The most beautiful thing we can experience is the mysterious. It is the source of all true art and science. He to whom this emotion is a stranger, who can no longer pause to wonder and stand rapt in awe, is as good as dead: his eyes are closed. This insight into the mystery of life, coupled though it be with fear, has also given rise to religion. To know that what is impenetrable to us really exists, manifesting itself as the highest wisdom and the most radiant beauty which our dull faculties can comprehend only in their most primitive form—this knowledge, this feeling, is at the center of true religiousness. In this sense, and in this sense only, I belong in the ranks of devoutly religious men. . . . It is enough for me to contemplate the mystery of conscious life perpetuating itself through all eternity, to reflect upon the marvelous structure of the universe which we can dimly perceive, and to try humbly to comprehend even an infinitesimal part of the intelligence manifested in nature."

—ALBERT EINSTEIN

"In so far as there are developments of thought that can be said to be characteristic of the twentieth century, the most powerful and impelling force behind them is the effort to break free of the nineteenth century and find a larger vision of reality."

—IRA PROGOFF

The essence of what I say in Part II is that man must become unencapsulated—at least relatively so—in order to find the larger vision of reality of which Progoff speaks in the quotation above. I suggest that the largeness of the vision is directly dependent upon how well modern man can break through the several psycho-epistemological cocoons within which he is encapsulated.

Life carries no guarantees, of course, so that mere movement away from unconsciousness will not necessarily bring about the millennium. But there is good reason to believe that greater awareness means the unlocking of the creative forces of the psyche, and that the release of free, creative energy, although it has its dangers, is conducive to the development of greater meaning in everyday living. Such heightening of existence would be symptomatic of the de-encapsulation process which will at least make it possible for larger visions to come into view in future generations.

6

The Development of Meaning

"Man's concern about a meaning of life is the truest expression of the state of being human."
—VIKTOR FRANKL

"The meaning of life is arrived at . . . by dark gropings, by feelings not wholly understood, by catching at hints and fumbling for explanations."
—ALFRED ADLER

In Part I of this book we have posed the dilemma of meaninglessness. We initiated the inquiry by tracing man's search for the ultimately real. We saw that each man is limited in that search, in fact that he is encapsulated, and that even when man is writ large he is finite when he comes to grips with himself and the universe. In spite of this, however, man has forged ways and means of understanding reality, but, to date, this effort has not led to a convergent end-point. In short, we have seen that the search for reality has led to epistemological relativism, that epistemological relativism results in value relativism, and that this lack of a clear-cut, absolute truth and absolute value has led 20th-century man to despair. But we ended the logical development of the dilemma of meaninglessness on an heroic note; we pointed out that there is an authenticity in the attitude of contemporary man which represents his most promising hope. We need to exploit this hope.

THE PSYCHOBIOLOGICAL BASIS OF MEANING

Let us begin with an investigation of the origin of meaning. This, of course, is not a small problem, and no matter where we initiate or end the inquiry, we will have to admit that we will have only made a beginning, and that our analysis will have been incomplete. Inquiries should, of course, begin at the beginning. But where is the beginning of the problem of meaning? Since I am approaching this at the level of the particular individual, that is, meaning for me, John Doe, it would seem reasonable to begin with the emergence of a John Doe into the world. But since the newborn who is to become John Doe comes into the world with certain constitutional equipment in the form of minute physico-chemical particles known as genes,[1] it is necessary for us to back up for just a moment before we pursue the development of this infant. The human being, after all, represents the highest known organic potential, and there might be some point in briefly reviewing his most probable origin:

(1) Somehow the first form of animal life, a one-celled animal probably not unlike the amoeba, came into existence. The best guess is that the environmental conditions were just right for the appropriate combination of physico-chemical events to produce raw protoplasm. When modern man learns how to synthesize protoplasm experimentally in the test tube, he will presumably have answered the question "What is life?"

(2) These early, amorphous globs of protoplasm reproduced themselves asexually via the potentiality of the genes.

(3) Over a period of perhaps hundreds of thousands of years, simple mutations occurred, broadening the varieties of protozoan structure. The phenotypes which fitted their environments survived; those that did not were eliminated according to the principle of natural selection.

(4) Over the 2 to 3 billion years of time since the origin of life on earth, through mutation and selection, there arose more and more complex organisms.

(5) Through isolation (geographic, climatic, environmental, reproductive, etc.) inbreeding resulted, producing unique species, sub-species, and other sub-groupings.

(6) This proliferation of animal life has eventuated in the human organism, *Homo sapiens*.

If we think of the evolutionary process in terms of passing from organic simplicity to relative complexity, we are immediately struck by the comparison between amoeba and man as representing the vast extremes of this protoplasmic continuum. In between these two species there are over a dozen phyla of the animal kingdom involving close to one million species of animal life. This represents a fantastic degree of variation, and the variation is rather intimately tied up with the effects of genes. The point I am making is this: the genes determine the constitutional equipment with which an organism emerges into the world. Each gene of the newborn is duplicated in the nucleus of each cell of the organism. And while all the details are by no means known, it is clear that genes do control the consequent structural and functional development of the organism. Let us cite specific examples of what we are saying. The human ear is capable of responding to sounds which range from 20 to 20,000 cycles per second, but the dog can hear sounds much beyond 20,000 cycles per second. The human eye is incapable of responding to infrared light waves. Human beings have varying eye color, hair color, and height. And some human beings (i.e., idiots, imbeciles), from birth, are unable to cope adequately with the environment because of inadequacies of brain function. Discounting the effects of nutritional deficiency, accidents, and other environmental variations, it is clear that genes determine the bodily equipment, the structure, with which the organism will interact in his physical and social environment. At the risk of being simple-minded, I am saying that it is the genes that are responsible for the dog zygote's developing into a dog and not a man. The genes, then, set the stage of life, they provide us with the machinery with which we are to work, and, while the overall design of this machine is the same for a given species, the variations within each species are very great. Human beings differ greatly in their biological equipment,[2] and these differences are bound to have an effect on the way each of us comes to grips with the environment.

The most important part of the total equipment of any organism is its coordinating units. And the most important of the several coordinating units of man is the nervous system, especially the brain. Even before the human organism emerges from his mother's womb, impulses have been registered in his relatively dormant brain. These include signals which emanate primarily from within the developing embryo itself, such as kinesthetic and proprioceptive cues, but they also include various tactual and other cues which are transmitted between the embryo and its limited environment, the mother's womb. While it has been demonstrated that very simple learning, for example, the conditioned response, can occur in the human fetus, the possibilities for meaningful contact between an embryo and the remainder of the universe are obviously rather limited.

After the human organism breaks the first bonds of encapsulation by emerging from the mother's womb, a much vaster world comes into view. With the aid of certain instinctive behavior patterns (e.g., such as sucking) which allow for survival, the human infant continues to grow and makes wider and wider contact with the external environment. Raw sounds and undifferentiated visual stimuli begin to pour into the brain. Complicated bodily movements occur. Behavior patterns literally unfold, and as Dr. Arnold Gesell has so ably demonstrated, the embryological processes of behavior, which had been occurring inside the mother's womb, continue outside the womb. With the increased maturity of sensory-motor and neural equipment, the learning process picks up in the form of many conditioned responses and simple trial-and-error learning. The conditioning process represents the first true sense of meaning, for we now have the internalization of "signs." That is, in the conditioned response, a new stimulus, the conditioned stimulus, evokes an old response. Hence, it is a "sign" or a cue for something with which one is familiar. Stated another way, in the classical Pavlovian experiment, we would say that the bell (conditioned stimulus), which is a "sign," "means" or "signifies" food (unconditioned stimulus).

With simple conditioning as a base, the human infant forages deeper into the forest of the unknown. He babbles, he moves, he sees and hears, he develops simple word concepts. He learns how to walk and talk, and he thinks and pokes around. He is a fantastically curious animal, and he learns with great rapidity. He learns that certain sound combinations will result in his being able to meet certain needs very simply, he learns that certain patterns of behavior will meet with approval and others with disapproval, he plays different roles as he gets older, and he eventually emerges as an adult member of society. We say he has been through "the socialization process," that is, he has consciously and unconsciously learned the language and behavior norms of a given social structure.

By adulthood, the human organism has internalized a way of looking at things, if you will, a "meaningful" way of looking at things, even if he says it all looks "meaningless." In the interaction process of organism with environment a major set of events has been continuously occurring which is optimally involved in the process of developing meaning. We place these events under the rubric of perception. Perception has to do with the way we see things. And we are suggesting that meaning is primarily a matter of how the organism "organizes" itself and the environment, and that perception is a focal point in this organizing process.

The essence of the answer to the question of how we perceive is that we perceive "*gestalts*." That is, we do not perceive a thousand and one minutiae as we gaze out of the window, the thousand and one minutiae which are there, but rather, we tend to see certain "wholes," certain total configurations, some of which we have perhaps named, such as tree, mountain, car, and house. Furthermore, depending upon the stimulus configuration and the direction of one's attention, a particular "form" or *gestalt* may temporarily stand out in one's consciousness. For example, as I gaze out of my window I am focusing on a small tree. In the background there are several houses, lawns, other trees, and shrubs, mountains, and sky. The dominant figure, the small tree, is referred to as the "figure," while we speak of the remaining somewhat undifferentiated mass as the "ground." There are certain "forces" in the visual field which tend to result in what the "gestaltists" call a "good figure." If the components of what is being perceived are simple, balanced, and symmetrical, it will tend to emerge as a clear-cut "figure" on a less differentiated "ground." Also, there are certain "groupings" and "closure" phenomena which contribute to the perception of "gestalts."

As an example, inspect the distribution of squares in Figure 8. We do not simply see 32 squares. First of all we see two big groups of 16 squares each. And then,

□ □ □ □   □ □ □ □

□ □ □ □   □ □ □ □

□ □ □ □   □ □ □ □

□ □ □ □   □ □ □ □

Fig. 8. The perceptual phenomenon of grouping

within each of the two groups, we see four groups of four squares. In the case of "closure," we simply "fill out" a given percept. Look at Figure 9. The typical response to this is that it represents a circle in spite of the fact

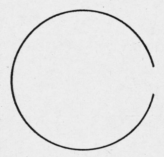

Fig. 9. The perceptual phenomenon of closure

that the drawing is incomplete. And, in fact, when this figure is tachistoscopically[3] presented, respondents are completely unaware of the fact that there is a discontinuity in the figure presented.

Recent work by G. S. Klein and his associates adds the dimension of personality to the basic perceptual processes just described. His point is that perception "is the point of reality contact, the door to reality appraisal, and there is no doubt that here especially are the selective, adaptive controls of personality brought into play."[4] He points out that a style of reality testing is revealed through certain perceptual attitudes. He posits three such attitudes, as follows: (1) leveling versus sharpening of differences; (2) resistance to or acceptance of instability; and (3) physiognomic and literal attitudes. The first attitude refers to the bringing out or ignoring of differences in what is perceived. Perceptual sharpeners tend to go toward objects and remain open to sensory inputs, whereas levelers are more likely to retreat from objects and the "outside world." The second attitude refers to tolerance of perceptual ambiguity, the willingness to accept formlessness in one's surroundings as opposed to the demand for a clear and well developed structure. The physiognomic attitude reflects the degree of affective distortion involved in the perceptual process. The implication is that the completely literal attitude would not involve any affect; such a person would presumably "see things exactly as they are." Klein offers these perceptual attitudes as personality-perceptual mechanisms which are comparable to the Freudian adjustment mechanisms. They can be properly conceived as homeostatic mechanisms—mechanisms of perceptual defense—brought into play to reduce tension in the process of adapting to the demands of life, particularly those demands we think of as cognitively "real" or "true."

THE CONCEPT OF STRUCTURE

Up to this point we have suggested that our evolutionary and genetic heritage, our subsequent physical and mental development, the learning process, the culture in which we have developed, and especially the process of perception are all involved in how the organism "organizes" itself and the environment. I suggest that all of these forces are manifestations of what I regard as the key concept for the development of meaning—namely, the concept of structure. I am suggesting that the manner in which structure is provided, outside and inside the organism, determines the meaning there is for the organism. The more amorphous the structure, for example, the less meaning there is. To the extent that there is organization or differentiation as opposed to homogeneity, there is meaning.[5] My thesis is that the concept of structure pervades everything, and that it is the clue to the problem of meaning. Let us develop this point in greater detail. Several examples from the domain of perception will help clarify what I am saying.

It is well known that pilots flying at great heights in a homogeneous blue sky have flown upside down without being aware of it. With the addition of certain cues, such as the perception of cloud formations, the normal kinesthetic pull of gravity when flying straight and level at a set speed in the upright position, looking at one's instruments, the perception of the earth, etc., such pilots were able to regain a sense of up-down orientation and subsequently maintain the normal flight pattern. Another example of perceptual confusion is the well known case of seeming to move while sitting in a stationary train adjacent to one that is moving slowly in the opposite direction. Most of us have had this sensation so forcefully as to be convinced that we were in fact moving, only to look out the opposite window and note that people and luggage were all quite stationary with respect to the position of the train. But the most convincing example of the importance of "structuring" the perceptual "field" occurs in the case of a fascinating illusion known as the autokinetic phenomenon. The autokinetic effect involves observing a stationary pinpoint of light in a completely darkened room. Most people report movement of the light source in spite of the fact that it does not actually move; hence the name, autokinetic, or self movement, phenomenon. This movement can be reduced or stopped completely by doing such things as increasing the light intensity of the room, flashing additional light sources into the visual field, or surrounding the autokinetic light with a concentric band of light.[6] In other words, by the addition of greater organization in the visual field, such as a "physical frame of reference" (e.g., a concentric band of light), the illusory movement is eliminated. Conversely, in a completely homogeneous black surround, a pinpoint of light cannot be anchored to anything else in the visual field (i.e., there is no frame of reference), and hence, it moves about aimlessly.

All three of these examples clearly show that meaning is dependent upon the structuring of the stimulus configuration. But earlier we stated that meaning depends upon both "outer" and "inner" organization. How does the "outer" organization become internalized? Fortunately the human organism is equipped with the symbolization machine *par excellence*—the brain. While there is undoubtedly more about the central nervous system which we do not know than we do know, we can at least indicate the broad outlines of how the brain internally structures its percepts. One thing which has been demonstrated rather clearly during the past quarter century is that the earlier analogy to a telephone switchboard is quite erroneous. It is acceptable as a description of the sensory input, motor output, simple reflex action, and possibly as a basis for the conditioned response, but it is completely misleading as a basis for such things as complex learning, perception, and thinking. The analogy to an electrical field of forces is more appropriate. That is, we know that electrical activity is going on in the brain at all times, and that this activity reflects the simultaneous electrical discharge of pools of neurons rather than the firing of neuron after neuron in a simple chain-linked arrangement. The electroencephalograph or brain-wave analyzer picks up synchronous wave patterns from the brain as a whole or from large segments. The pattern of activity looks the same when taken from adjacent points. In other words, electroencephalography and other evidence indicates that the ten billion neurons of the brain tend to resonate in accordance with an overall field of forces—a *gestalt* of electrical activity which determines the activity of the parts, rather than the reverse. This type of evidence is consistent with the findings of Lashley on mass action, as well as the findings on vicarious functioning, which indicate that remaining cortical tissue can frequently take over the functions which were previously handled by excised neural tissue. The story of mass action versus localization of function in the brain is a vast and confusing one. The evidence is mixed, and it is impossible to make an unqualified generalization about just how the higher mental functions are neurologically mediated. But in spite of the confusion, there does seem to be convincing evidence to indicate that the brain is organized for flexibility, that there are a multitude of routes and connections, and that neural firing at the cortical level is a matter of pooled synchronicity rather than individual firing as in the periphery. Perhaps this pooled synchronicity or electrical field can best be explained by the analogy of dropping a pebble into a pool of still water. We note that a wave of excitation fans out from the point at which the pebble entered the smooth surface. If we do this at regular intervals, we can record a definite rhythmic wave action, reflecting the turbulence of the pool of water. Similarly, the application of electrodes to the skull, and the subsequent recording of electrical activity of the brain on several writing mechanisms, reveals the normal 10 cycles per second alpha rhythm of the awakened, rested, human brain, the 4 c.p.s. delta rhythm of the sleeping brain, and the 10 c.p.s., low-amplitude kappa rhythm of the thinking brain. Thus, we see that the brain is organized in terms of electrical fields of force.

The nervous system is also organized in terms of receptors, which are neural structures, specialized in terms of the kind of stimuli they will allow into the organism. For example, the retina of the eye can handle light waves, but it cannot respond to sound waves; the rods and cones *in situ* respond to chemical stimulation but not to thermal stimulations; and so forth. Once stimulated, either chemically, thermally, mechanically, electrically, or photically, the sensory input neurons simply conduct the neural impulse. All neural impulses are the same, an electrochemical neutralization process which moves with great speed from one adjacent point of the neuron to the next, regardless of the nature or the point of origin of the initial stimulation. But all incoming impulses, via the eye, the ear, the skin, kinesthetic input, etc., converge on a central pool of ongoing electrical activity in the brain. That is, incoming neural impulses do not enter a silent, central switchboard. Rather, incoming impulses flow into a heavy traffic center, comparable to Broadway or 42nd Street. What we have, then, is a highly flexible, fluid, dynamic situation, with certain definite structures in the periphery, such as eyes, ears, and muscles; certain important control points such as ganglia and the medulla oblongata, which are areas for the control of vital activities such as breathing; and key areas such as the thalamus and the midbrain, which are way stations for the integration of large segments of behavior such as emotional expression. All of these centers feed into and out of the cortex, which we can think of as a vast, six-layered electrical field dynamically concerned with maintaining a state of equilibrium.

How can such a system allow for the amazing order of which we know the brain to be capable? The *gestalt* psychologists have provided us with a highly insightful clue with their concept of isomorphism. Isomorphism simply means sameness of structure. And, as it relates to neuropsychology, the concept means that there is an electrical representation of neural events in the brain which is comparable to a specific psychological percept. In other words, there is a functional representation in the brain which corresponds to a specific structural arrangement at the phenomenological or behavioral level. Perhaps a brief description of a famous experiment by Wolfgang Köhler[7] will be helpful at this juncture. Köhler had subjects view a large drawing of a cross. He attached many electrodes to all parts of the occipital cortex, the back portion of the brain which mediates visual function. He would flash the diagram of the cross on and off. While the symbol of the cross was on he was able to pick up a certain brain-wave pattern; when the cross was not presented he simply got the normal alpha rhythm. In other words, that particular electrical activity of the brain was the neurological isomorph of the figure we call a cross. Similarly the previously mentioned kappa rhythm is the neurological isomorph for a certain type of thinking activity. It should be noted that the similarity of structure between the neural and experiential levels does not require absolute equivalence, although this is not ruled out. All that is required is that there be a topological equivalence, that is, that a particular portion of the phenomenological structure correspond to a particular portion of the neural structure (e.g., as a rubber map may be stretched in a variety of ways without destroying relative position).

Must we confine the concept of structure to perception? Obviously not, otherwise we should not be able to offer a sufficiently broad base for the comprehension of meaning. Piaget, a Swiss psychologist, believes the con-

cept of structure pervades all thought, from the first
sensory-cortical input of the infant to the unified field
theory of the physicist. In a lifetime series of experimental
researches on the thought process of the child [8] he demonstrates the importance of "mental structures" in re-
acting to the external environment. He points out, for
example, that new objects presented to the infant by the
external environment can only be responded to in terms
of a "mental structure" that has to do with sucking,
looking, or grasping. Thus, if presented with a one hundred dollar bill, the infant would be more likely to stuff
it in his mouth than in his pocket. His "internal structure," essentially sucking, looking, or grasping, simply does
not include the economic evaluating structure of the
adolescent or the adult. Piaget has also demonstrated the
importance of internal structuring as a determinant of
the ability of children to make a proper induction when
exposed to a standard problem. Take, for example, the
problem of determining the number of eggs and egg cups
under each of three conditions: (1) placing an egg opposite each cup, (2) crowding the eggs into a small space
as opposed to stretching out the display of cups, and
(3) reversing the latter situation. Piaget found that when
the eggs were placed opposite the cups the children concluded that there were not as many eggs as cups, but
whatever was bunched together in a small space was seen
as fewer in number. These and other examples demonstrate Piaget's point that the qualitative level of the response is dependent upon the developmental level (i.e.,
the "mental structure") of the subject.

At this point Piaget's concepts of assimilation and accommodation are relevant, for these two processes are
seen as the major adaptive mechanisms in structuring the
world. By assimilation Piaget means the process of relating the new to the present cognitive structure of the
person. By accommodation he means the necessity of responding to the new by a change in the present structure
of the person. Whereas assimilation is essentially conserving and ego-centered, accommodation is essentially radical
and object-centered. Adapting to the world is a balance
and interaction between assimilation and accommodation,
when the organism is sometimes dominated by the process

of assimilation, and at other times is more open to new inputs. Thus, in early life, the child proceeds primarily by way of assimilation, meeting his basic needs rather directly and with little or no awareness of the separateness of himself and his surround. At this stage he is simply not ready for the fine discriminations which the process of accommodation will foster. His "mental structure" is such that he can only respond instinctively or reflexly, with little or no flexibility or awareness. As the infant develops psychobiologically, and as the demands of the environment increase, more and more accommodations become necessary. As the accommodations become more effective, the originally antagonistic interplay between assimilation and accommodation is replaced by a mutuality and a complementariness which lead to an increased facility for taking in more and more of the outside world. Psychologically, such a development implies a growth from an essentially subjective outlook on life to a more objective viewpoint. Piaget sees the latter as reflecting a more mature "mental structure."

Perhaps the most interesting aspect of Piaget's work on structure is the parallel he sees between one's personal "mental structure" and the scientist's theoretical structure of the universe. Take, for example, Piaget's description of the child's and the scientist's conception of space:

> The sky seems to us as a big spherical or elliptical cover on whose surface move images without depth which alternately interpenetrate and detach themselves: sun and moon, clouds. . . . It is only through patient observations relating the movements of these images and the way they mask each other, that we arrive at the kind of elaborating subjective groups which satisfied mankind until the constitution of objective groups was made possible by the Copernican image of the earth and the solar system. At first, with regard to immediate perception, there exist neither conscious groups nor permanent solids (the celestial bodies seen to be re-absorbed into each other and not to hide behind one another), nor even depth; there is only accommodation of eyes, head, and body which enables us to follow the movement of some cloud or of the moon, or to perceive a faint star, but the practical groups which we thus utilize are not yet extended into any subjective group. . . . The child's whole space considered from the point of view of distances

is analogous to the celestial space of immediate perception
which we have just described: a fluid man without depth
. . . traversed by images which interpenetrate or become
detached without laws and alternately separate and re-
unite. . . .[9]

A comparable objectification of the visual field occurs for
the young child as he interacts with objects in the external
environment and particularly as he develops a need to
communicate such representations to others. Piaget suggests that a similar evolution from sensorimotor to conceptual thought occurs with other major variables of life
such as causality and time. Piaget's evidence drives him
to the suggestion that "the (child's) completion of the
objective practical universe resembles Newton's achievements as compared to the egocentrism of Aristotelian
physics, but the absolute Newtonian time and space themselves remain egocentric from the point of view of
Einstein's relativity because they envisage only one perspective on the universe among many other perspectives
which are equally possible and real." [10] Thus, all thought
starts with instinctive-like assimilation and moves on to
an egocentric accommodation, primarily in terms of personal affect rather than "objective truth." In its advanced
stages, the subject-object distinction becomes clearer, the
necessity for everything revolving around "me" becomes
less and less plausible or defensible, and a less egocentric
world-view finally emerges. Piaget's point is that individual
autogeny and the maturity of a science seem to go through
the same basic stages.

We have seen how the concept of structure tends to
order the environment, the perceptual field, and the
processes of the brain. We also saw that the genes with
which we enter the world determine a bodily structure
for us, including our brains. Our brains are then further
structured in terms of the conditioning process, the culture which is subsequently internalized, and the processes
of perception. As we mature, both individually and as a
culture, an ideology finally emerges. If this ideology refers
to a scientific discipline, we speak of it as a theoretical
framework. Consider, for example, the obvious theoretical
structure of the field of chemistry in which one combines
elements, makes diagrams showing valences and bonds,

etc., in order to reveal the structure of compounds. Similarly, the theoretical structure of any scientific discipline is the ultimate goal toward which each science is striving, for it is this structure which provides meaning for the factual observations which are thereby integrated. In a very real sense all we have in mathematics is structure; perhaps it would not be incorrect to think of the discipline of mathematics as structure in the abstract. It is precisely because of the abstractness or emptiness of mathematics that its structure is so ubiquitously capable of moving into a chaotic empirical domain and ordering it. Mathematics as such—that is, pure mathematics— deals with abstract relations without regard to content. Such a lattice work is capable, however, of handling whatever content will fit, be it the experimental observations of nuclear physics or the social behavior of monkeys. Mathematics is therefore the ultimate language of theoretical science, the most comprehensive and "meaningful" way to structure the many previously unrelated phenomenal bits. With this perspective we can also see a heretofore not too obvious parallel between mathematics and art, for in art we are also concerned with structure, sometimes abstract, sometimes not. The most obvious parallel in this context is with music, for it is, in general, the most abstract of the major art forms. It is also the most mathematical-like of the various arts, with its symbols and its demand that this complex structure of symbols be, in some way, internally consistent. But the emphasis on structure or form is the essence of all art. In fact, if an artistic product is too unstructured or formless, it ceases to convey anything, and it merges into the same meaningless pattern as formlessness in any other aspect of life. One of the difficult problems of modern and abstract art, of course, is to decipher the new form which the artist has introduced. If it is impossible for respondents to identify this form, it simply misfires as art. Such misfiring may be due either to inadequacies of the artistic product itself, or to the respondent. If it is due to the respondent, it is a matter of becoming educated, able to appreciate a new way of looking at reality. In such instances the new art form somehow touches reality, thereby reflecting truth. Such art products represent true art, art which is universal; such art eventually finds a responsive audience. But if the deficiency lies with the artistic product, then the misfiring must lie with the artist. I suggest that in such cases his artistic products are too idiosyncratic, which means he projects a structure which is too subjective, merely a small quirk of the artist's personality rather than a reflection of reality. Such efforts misfire as art because of the lack of universality in their structure.

The structuring of the world is similar in all of man's approaches to reality, whether it be through science or art. But, in both cases the particular structure which emerges will reflect reality only if it is somehow universal. In science this universality is reached by a congruence of repeatable empirical findings with the predictions of a theoretical structure. In art this universality is reached only if the artist transcends himself by creating art which goes beyond mere subjectivity and is capable of standing as a statement for mankind. It is interesting to note that subjectivity is involved in both endeavors, but that the artist has a more difficult epistemological problem. For the scientist, as scientist, has a more efficient external machinery for correcting his subjective structures, whereas the artist, while able to be more experimental and creative about the structures he imposes on life, runs the greater risk that his efforts will turn out to be merely subjective —that is, too idiosyncratic, and thereby unable to unveil reality. Great art, on the other hand, unveils reality of which science cannot speak, primarily because of its openness to the production of a greater variety of new forms and new ways to structure reality.

Structuring the world is manifest in all man's activities, especially in those activities which have achieved a high degree of cultural sophistication, such as the arts and sciences. If the structuring process refers to one's philosophy of life, then we are dealing with the question we started with at the beginning of this chapter, namely, "Where does meaning come from?" Our answer is that it comes about as a function of structure, within the person, outside him, and in the organism-environment interaction. And, as we shall see in the next chapter, the key to personal meaning lies in the structure of each individual's epistemological and value hierarchies.

NOTES

1. There is convincing evidence that the essential genetic material is a nucleic acid called desoxyribonucleic acid, or DNA. This material is believed to be the basis for the specific chemical reactions of genes. See G. W. Beadle, The gene: carrier of heredity, controller of function and agent of evolution, *Nieuevland Lecturer in Chemistry and Biology*, University of Notre Dame, 1955, 7, 1-24, and J. D. Watson and F. H. C. Crick, The structure of DNA, *Cold Spring Symposia on Quantitative Biology*, 1953, 18, 123.

2. Roger Williams, *Biochemical Individuality*, New York: Wiley, 1956.

3. A tachistoscope is a standard gadget in the psychology laboratory which allows the investigator to present a stimulus for a specifiable period of time. Thus, its greatest value is in the "flash" presentation of stimuli in the study of perception and learning.

4. G. S. Klein, The personal world through perception. In R. Blake and G. Ramsey, *Perception: An Approach to Personality*, New York: Ronald Press, 1951, pp. 328-329.

5. In this connection it is important to note that this conception need not remain as a purely theoretical construction, for the recent publication of W. R. Garner's book, *Uncertainty and Structure as Psychological Concepts*, New York: John Wiley and Sons, 1962, provides us with a convincing theoretical-empirical development of the concept of structure. Garner points out that meaning as structure can be quantified via the growing machinery of information theory. Thus, we can anticipate more direct empirical tests of the claims I make in this section.

6. The writer is currently pursuing a research project on this problem under the title "Experimental Reduction of Autokinetic Movement." See, for example, a publication under the above title in the *American J. of Psychology*, 1962, 75, 221-231.

7. Wolfgang Köhler and R. Held, The cortical correlate of pattern vision, *Science*, 1949, 110, 414-419.

8. See, for example, J. Piaget, *The Child's Conception of the World*, London: Routledge and Kegan Paul, 1929, and *The Construction of Reality in the Child*, New York: Basic Books, 1954.

9. J. Piaget, *The Construction of Reality in the Child*, New York: Basic Books, pp. 144-145.

10. *Ibid.*, p. 367.

7

Meaning, Value, and Personality

"This above all: to thine own self be true. And it must follow, as the night the day, Thou canst not then be false to any man."

—SHAKESPEARE

". . . make the most of (life): put into it all you have got, and live and, if possible, die with some measure of nobility."

—WILLIAM KAUFMAN

"Whatever things have intimate and continuous connection with my life are things of whose reality I cannot doubt. Whatever things fail to establish the connection are things which are practically no better for me than if they existed not at all."

—WILLIAM JAMES

When we talk about a man's personality, we are trying to capture something of his essence as a human being, his major traits or characteristics, what he typically does or says, his major beliefs, and so forth. If we probe deeply into a personality we find a man's self concept at the core. By self concept we mean what a man thinks of himself when the façade of social living has been removed. The man who has a clear view of himself is said to have a strong ego or a strong personality. We say that he knows who he is and that he knows where he has been and where he is going. The confused personality, on the other hand, does not know who he is. His self concept is vague or chameleon-like. He shifts with the personalities or the events which surround him, and when one probes to the depths of his personality, one finds little or nothing there. In the previous chapter we tried to show how personal meaning develops out of a complicated interaction between the individual and his environment. The concept of organization or structure was developed as the central idea.

THE PSYCHO-EPISTEMOLOGICAL PROFILE
AND THE VALUE HIERARCHY

The bridge between meaning and personality is value.
The key to a man's self concept, or the meaning he places
on life, is his value system. Each man has a value hierarchy, a scale of values which he follows as a guide or
framework for ordering his behavior. For example, the
missionary places religious values higher than economic
values, whereas the business man may reverse these.
Academicians and scientists stake their meaning on theoretical values, artists stress the esthetic, and politicians
identify with power. Each of these terms—religious, theoretical, economic, power—reflects a broad evaluative
attitude. That is, the "theoretical man" tends to be highly
systematic and orderly, the "economic man" wants everything to be practical, and the "esthetic man" sees his
highest value in beauty. Because of its importance to our
subsequent discussion I am going to spell out each of
these value systems in greater detail. The descriptions
which follow are taken from the Allport-Vernon-Lindzey
Study of Values,[1] one of the few available efforts to study
values empirically. These authors point out that their
investigation is based on a philosophical work of Edouard
Spranger, titled *Types of Men*. The six value systems
follow:

Theoretic. The dominant interest of the theoretical man
is the discovery of truth. In the pursuit of this goal he characteristically takes a cognitive attitude, one that looks for
identities and differences; one that divests itself of judgments
regarding the beauty or utility of objects, and seeks only to
observe and to reason. Since the interests of the theoretical
man are empirical, critical, and rational, he is necessarily an
intellectualist, frequently a scientist or philosopher. His chief
aim in life is to order and to systematize his knowledge.

Economic. The economic man is characteristically interested in what is useful. Based originally upon the satisfaction
of bodily needs (self-preservation), the interest in utilities
develops to embrace the practical affairs of the business world,
the production, marketing and consumption of goods, the
elaboration of credit, and the accumulation of tangible
wealth. This type is thoroughly practical and conforms well

to the prevailing conception of the average American businessman.

Aesthetic. The aesthetic man sees his highest value in form and harmony. Each single experience is judged from the standpoint of grace, symmetry, or fitness. He regards life as a manifold of events; each single impression is enjoyed for its own sake. He need not be a creative artist; nor need he be effete; he is aesthetic if he but finds his chief interest in the artistic episodes of life.

Social. The highest value for this type is love of people, whether of one or many, whether conjugal, filial, friendly, or philanthropic. The social man prizes other persons as ends, and is therefore himself kind, sympathetic, and unselfish. He is likely to find the theoretical, economic, and aesthetic attitudes cold and inhuman. In contrast to the political type, the social man regards love as itself the only suitable form of power, or else repudiates the entire conception of power as endangering the integrity of personality. In its purest form the social interest is selfless and tends to approach very closely to the religious attitude.

Political. The political man is interested primarily in power. His activities are necessarily within the narrow field of politics; but whatever his vocation he portrays himself as a *Macht Mensch.* Leaders in any field generally have a high power value. Since competition and struggle play a large part in all life, many philosophers have seen power as the most universal and most fundamental of motives.

Religious. The highest value for the religious man may be called unity. He is mystical, and seeks to comprehend the cosmos as a whole, to relate himself to its embracing totality. Spranger defines the religious man as one "whose mental structure is permanently directed to the creation of the highest and absolutely satisfying value experience!"

It is unfortunate that only six value systems are available for study, for surely there are more. But in spite of this limitation, behavior scientists have accumulated convincing evidence which shows that while each man invests in a variety of values, he tends to relegate those needs which are least important for him (important in terms of the preservation of one's self concept) to the bottom of the value hierarchy, and to elevate those values which are most important to him to the apex of his hierarchy. In Figure 10, for example, we have indicated the average

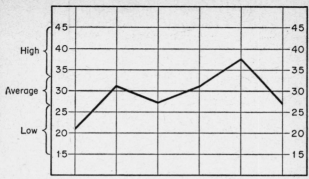

Fig. 10. Value profile of 51 male law students

value profile of 51 male law students on the Study of Values. This profile indicates that political values lie at the apex of the lawyer's value hierarchy, with economic and social values tied at the next level, with religious and esthetic values next, and with theoretical values at the bottom of this hierarchy. Let us contrast this with the value profile of literature students. In Figure 11 we see

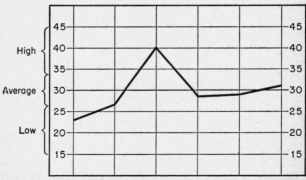

Fig. 11. Value profile of 24 female literature students

that the typical literature student places esthetic values at the apex of his hierarchy, with religion in the second slot, political, social, and economic next, and with theoretical values in last place. The contrast in the priority of esthetic values for the literature student as opposed to the priority of political values for the law student is obvious and, I should think, to be expected from what is general knowledge concerning these contrasted groups. Other findings on the Allport-Vernon-Lindsey indicate that, in general, males tend to be slightly above average on theoretical, economical, and political values, and slightly below average on aesthetic, social, and religious values. Females show the reverse pattern.

Recent experimental research in psychology has brought out some provocative relationships beween values and the way we perceive. In one experiment, for example, Bruner and Goodman[3] showed that children from poor homes tended to see a low-valued coin, such as a nickel, as a half dollar. Rich children, on the other hand, tended toward the reverse, namely, to see half-dollar coins as nickels. In another study[4] the investigators made use of the Allport-Vernon-Lindsey inventory as their point of departure. They selected a total of 36 stimulus words to represent each of the six value orientations of the Study of Values. These words were flash presented (i.e., tachistoscopically in hundredths of a second) to subjects whose value hierarchies had been determined by the Study of Values. Each word was presented at varying intervals of time until it was correctly perceived. In general, those words which reflected one's value preference were most readily perceived, whereas those words which reflected a lesser value preference required longer exposure times for correct perception.

These and similar reports have provided experimental confirmation for what has long been suspected in the psychological clinic—that values and motivational needs serve as important determinants of how and what we perceive. This is, after all, the thinking which lies behind such clinical instruments as the Rorschach Inkblot cards, which are purposely vague visual stimulus configurations. The theory is that the subject, via perceptual-personality mechanisms that are not well understood, will project various aspects of his deepest personality structure on to these vague perceptual stimuli. This projected material will include responses which reflect motivational and value facets of the personality. In short, a variety of experimental and clinical findings indicate a "resonance" of cognitive functioning with the values that the individual holds. The writer regards these findings as consistent with the four approaches to reality presented in Chapter 2. The point is that values are important determinants of one's perceptual attitude or frame of reference. If, for example, one places a greater value upon logic than upon empirical observation, then one is more likely to "see things" in terms of the psycho-epistemological approach of rationalism than empiricism. A similar argument can be made for each of the four approaches to reality. Further, just as there is a value hierarchy which reflects an individual's implicit or explicit value system, there is also (I am hypothesizing) a psycho-epistemological hierarchy which reflects how an individual structures reality. This implies that a given individual characteristically relies more on one or two of the basic approaches to reality than upon the others. The typical scientist, for example, would be likely to have empiricism and rationalism at the top of his profile, with intuitionism and authoritarianism at the bottom. The laboratory man's profile might read: empiricism, rationalism, intuitionism, and authoritarianism. The theoretician's profile would be the same except for a reversal of rationalism and empiricism. A highly creative theoretician, however, might have a profile as follows: rationalism, intuitionism, empiricism, and authoritarianism. Artists, in general, would have a profile with intuitionism near the apex. And an ardent member of a fundamentalist religious group would reflect a profile somewhat as follows: authoritarianism, empiricism, rationalism, intuitionism. The writer has initiated research along these lines, but it is too early to tell to what extent the data will confirm our expectations.[5] In any event, the implications of this line of development are that there are a variety of approaches to reality, that the psychobiological history of each individual determines how he will implicitly or explicitly rank each of the four epistemologies, and that any one approach is by definition limited, thereby reflecting an encapsulated view of reality.

The inevitable fact of encapsulation as it relates to values and our conceptions of reality raises the question of how best to invest in values. Among other findings, modern depth psychology reveals that many neurotics do not invest wisely in their value systems. That is, the neurotic fails in the business of "becoming" because he does not establish a clear value hierarchy, or, he adopts one which is alien to his nature, and the result is that there is little potential for personal growth and fulfillment. This has been a favorite theme in literature, and it will undoubtedly continue to be in the future, for it reflects a perennial failure of man. This theme is evident in occasional short stories, novels, or plays of past centuries, such as Guy de Maupassant's *The Necklace*,[6] where a lifetime is wasted on paying off a necklace which turns out to have been imitation; or in Chekhov's *Cherry Orchard*,[7] where a group of aristocrats are identified with a clear enough value hierarchy, but the values in which they invest are no longer viable. Nowhere is the emptiness and horror of misplaced values more potently portrayed than in Tolstoy's *The Death of Ivan Ilytch*. Here is a man who had been content with himself all his life. He had achieved reasonable material success and had served well as a high court judge. He is severely ill, and in fact, is dying. The meaninglessness of death and, worse yet, of his personal life, forces itself upon his last days of consciousness. He says, for example:

> "What do I want? To live and not to suffer. . . . To live? How? . . . Why, to live as I used to—well and pleasantly." "As you lived before, well and pleasantly?" the voice persisted. And in imagination he began to recall the best moments of his pleasant life. But strange to say none of those best moments of his pleasant life now seemed at all what they had then seemed. . . . And the further he departed from childhood and the nearer he came to the present the more worthless and doubtful were the joys. . . . "It is as if I had been going downhill while I imagined I was going up. And that is really what it was. I was going up in public opinion, but to the same extent life was ebbing away from me. And now it is all done and there is only death." . . . "Maybe I did not live as I ought to have done." "But how could that be, when I did everything properly?"

he replied, and immediately dismissed from his mind this, the sole solution of all the riddle of life and death, as something quite impossible. . . . And whenever the thought occurred to him, as it often did, that it all resulted from his not having lived as he ought to have done, he at once recalled the correctness of his whole life and dismissed so strange an idea.[8]

Finally Ivan Ilytch somehow gains insight into himself and faces the fact that he has invested in a value schema which for him was essentially empty, for he says that "his professional duties and the whole arrangement of his life and his family, and all his social and official interests, might all have been false. He tried to defend all those things to himself and suddenly felt the weakness of what he was defending. There was nothing to defend. . . . All you have lived for and still live for is falsehood and deception, hiding life and death from you."[9]

Such a theme, however, is most likely to receive its best development in periods of value transition such as the present century. Therefore, many potent examples come from contemporary literature. Take, for example, Charles Gray in J. P. Marquand's *Point of No Return*.[10] Gray realizes a lifelong ambition, the vice-presidency of a bank, only to discover that his essentially materialistically oriented goals are not what he really wants. Through a lifetime of little choices he ends up essentially unfulfilled in any deep sense, and in the end he is forced to the conclusion that he has reached "the point of no return." John Phillips, in *The Second Happiest Day*,[11] warns us that we had best choose carefully, for we may get what we think we want. In this dramatization the hero willingly and very readily sells out for material and social advantages, even in the face of having to put up with a wife who will give him a life of hell. She is part of the deal, however, and what's more, he is under the impression that he really wants her. Both the wife and the job represent "success" of an external sort, but he is willing to sacrifice everything else for these all-important goals. An opposite kind of value confusion is brought out in *The Man in the Gray Flannel Suit*.[12] In this novel the hero allows his talents and abilities to lie fallow. He refuses to work at the high level of which he is capable because he does not want to risk what he's already got. In short, he sells out to security and safety, a value orientation which may characterize the present post-World War II, cold-war generation.

Perhaps the most potent example of this theme from contemporary literature, however, is that of Willy Loman in Arthur Miller's *The Death of a Salesman*.[13] Here is a man who thinks the most important thing in the world is to be liked. He wants to be a "big man," and he sees the job of a traveling salesman as the way for him to reach this station. At the end of his life Willy comes to the realization that his life has been empty, that his ambitions were all external, that meaning has escaped him. The irony of his great concern for how he affected others was that most of his "friends" actually did not care for him. And the irony of his eagerness to be a "big man" was his realization that he was literally worth more dead than alive. He finds a type of meaning in the money his death will make available to his family. One of his sons, Biff, fortunately unlearns what his father had taught him, and decides to go to work on a ranch out west simply because that's what he likes best. The younger son, Happy, tragically follows in his father's footsteps, intent on beating "the system" and vindicating his father's beliefs, a thorough convert to the power of "the big front" as the way to success, happiness, being liked, and becoming a "big man." All of these literary characters are looking for the same thing—justification as a human being, the depth of meaning which follows from an investment in values which are consistent with one's individuality.

We also see many examples of misplaced values on the contemporary American scene, as in the case of the journalist who prints scandal material in order to sell newspapers or magazines, the public official who thinks he is gaining national security by requiring loyalty oaths, and the educator who replaces the value of intellectual rigor with the norm of "adjustment." [14] What does all this show? Essentially, an inability to uphold, or to find, the more intrinsic value. The educator knows that his main concern is with scholarship, but he sells out to a non-scholarly value, adjustment. And the result is a concomitant decrease in the meaning or significance of contemporary American education. That is, we do not think much of "adjustment" as scholarship, just as we are not convinced that very many newspapers are interested in "truth" or that signing loyalty oaths is the way to maintain a democratic society. Unfortunately, the cumulative effect is a decline in the "progress" of our society.

When this loss in meaning occurs at the individual level the person loses self-respect. He does not think very much of the "self" he sees. One way to meet this situation is to avoid looking at one's self as much as possible; in effect, to avoid the problem of "becoming." Thus we emerge with the unexamined value system. We have a human being who refuses to live out a life which is consistent with his "inner" meaning. We need a reaffirmation of individualism and depth probing in contemporary life. We need individuals who will be willing and proud to be themselves, to be "normal" in the more mature sense of "becoming," who recognize the fact that one loses personal integrity and wholeness unless he adheres to a value system which is consistent with his uniqueness. Only as a man lives out this uniqueness can he unlock the creative potential that is latent within him. The release and development of creativity is the greatest single resource known to mankind, for its nurturing leads to fullness of being in both the sense of meaning for the individual and progress for civilization. I am not speaking here of the creativity of the painter, the composer, or the writer, but rather of "everyman" as he creates himself.

Here is one of the places where the existentialists have a valid lesson for mankind, for they insist that man chooses his own values, and there is considerable evidence from the behavioral sciences to support this view. That is, the new-born embryo is not born with a value system; rather, the value hierarchy is learned over the years (on top of a genetic structure, of course) as an important aspect of the process of socialization. And as a differentiated personality structure begins to emerge, the way the individual structures his values stands out as the key to his personality. If he develops a value hierarchy which is consistent with his inner nature, his capacities, his goals, the center of his being, he has set the stage for creative personality development. But if he tries to take on values which are inconsistent with his inner nature, he has sown the seeds for a constricted or distorted personality.

PSYCHOLOGY, EXISTENTIALISM, AND RELIGION: TOWARD A COMMON THEORY OF MAN

Unfortunately, modern psychology has not paid sufficient attention to the importance of values in personality development. Laboratory psychology is largely incapable of tackling the problem (except for the "new look" research on perception and values mentioned at the beginning of this chapter), psychometric theory has made the barest beginnings in measuring a person's value hierarchy, and psychoanalysis has been overly preoccupied with the vagaries of unconscious motivation. Because of a dearth of factual information and the impact of a variety of other biases, relatively little interest in the problem of values has been shown by our applied students of personality, the psychotherapists. The anthropologically oriented social psychoanalysts, such as Karen Horney and Erich Fromm, have been aware of the condition of contemporary society, but they have been too steeped in the orthodoxy of psychoanalysis to depart significantly from Freudian procedures in therapy.

Perhaps the most provocative recent developments in the psychology of values comes from certain isolated Europeans who have been referred to as existential psychologists and psychiatrists.[15] Of this group the work which deals most explicitly with the existential aspects of values is that of the late Werner Wolff. In his book *Values and Personality*, he includes a verbatim record of two cases of existential neurosis. Here we see that as a therapist Wolff does not concern himself with childhood traumas, the oedipus complex, and anal or oral fixations. He seems more interested in the perceptions which challenge his clients' existence—"those difficult events, thoughts and circumstances which produce dread, anxiety, and disturbance." In other words, he presses for the patient's value hierarchy. In the process he hopes to aid his client to a greater awareness of his values, and to force him to face the problem of what it means to exist in terms of them.

We see here the same concern for authenticity, for living out one's life genuinely, honestly, with depth and awareness, which the existential philosopher espouses. Wolff says, for example, that man ". . . tries to escape from any existential tension. . . . The task of existential therapy is to give the individual insight into his existential reality, to unify his individuality, and to make him able to face the responsibilities of the existential risk." [16] Tillich speaks of this unwillingness to face the existential risk as the lost dimension of depth in the religious quest and devotes a whole book to the importance of the courage to become one's self.[17] Whether or not we have the courage to "be," each of us "is," and as Gordon Allport points out, we spend a lifetime "becoming." [18] Becoming what? Why, becoming what we were meant to become, of course. Becoming in terms of innate capacities, personal and social needs, and most importantly, "becoming" in terms of our "value hierarchies." Every man, says Allport, "whether he is religiously inclined or not, has his own ultimate presuppositions. He finds he cannot live his life without them, and for him they are true. Such presuppositions, whether they be called ideologies, philosophies, notions, or merely hunches about life, exert creative pressure upon all conduct. . . ." [19]

Allport is one of the few psychologists of repute to speak out so boldly and forcefully on religion.[20] There have been other efforts, such as those of Clark,[21] Johnson,[22] Mowrer,[23] and Maslow,[24] but there has been no sustained, unified concern on the part of psychologists. Psychology and religion have, of course, a long and well known history of mutual indifference and, at times, animosity. Psychologists, concerned with the scientific status of their discipline, have felt that identification with a humanistic discipline such as religion would sell out psychology's cause before it had a chance to come into existence as a science. Religionists, on the other hand, have traditionally feared scientific advances because of the apparent widening encroachment of alien fields. The history of the rift between various sciences and religion clearly demonstrates that a rapprochement eventually develops. This rapprochement follows automatically when each contender comes to the realization that his opponent, while formidable, is not sufficient in isolation, and is therefore not impregnable. With the door thus opened, each is more ready to learn from the other. Each contender sees the positive contributions of the other, and because of this each is more ready to join forces in the search for truth.

There are signs that the beginnings of a rapprochement between psychology and religion are occurring. In particular, I am thinking of the recent establishment of the "working group" on psychology and religion. (See Acknowledgments, page vi, for names of participants.) This group is particularly interested in studying the basic presuppositions of psychology and religion, and the relations between the two. But perhaps the outstanding development along these lines is that of pastoral psychology. However, it must be admitted that this development is due more to the openness of the religionists than it is to the combined efforts of both disciplines. It is to be hoped that these expressions of a more positive attitude on the part of both religion and psychology represent a beginning of intensive and open study of problems of mutual interest. For our concern is not with the practical problems of interdisciplinary diplomacy, but rather, with the development of an all-encompassing theory of man. Such a goal will require the insights of all students of man, whether they come from the scientific or the humanistic camp. The psychiatrists (e.g., Jung) and social psychoanalysts (e.g., Fromm) have been much more open to religious thought than have the psychologists. However, I predict a change in psychology along these lines in the near future. This prediction is based primarily on the impact of existentialism on 20th-century thought. There are indications that this approach to man is not being taken lightly in spite of its essentially non-systematic form, and that it contains religious insights which make sense to both religionists and scientists. The purpose of this section is to point up the relevance of existentialism to both psychology and religion, with the idea of offering it as an intellectual bridge between the two.

Because of the richness of each domain, the potential lines of convergence between psychology, existentialism, and religion are many. However, it must be admitted that the points of overlap are fuzzy and confused. The material which follows, therefore, is to be regarded primarily as suggestive and exploratory. Furthermore, stress will be placed on a discursive exposition of the contributions from existentialism which may be common or at least relevant to the other two. No attempt will be made to exhaustively and systematically interrelate all three domains. It should be obvious that even this relatively limited task is beyond the capabilities of an exponent from only one of the three domains.

Let us begin with several observations which are common to all three approaches. Perhaps the idea which all three disciplines share most completely is that for self-realization each man must live authentically. Here we are dealing with the problem of values and what it means to live out one's life in terms of them. This concern is most obviously identified with religion, with its traditional stress on investing in those values which have the potential of supplying sufficient meaning to sustain the full life. A similar concern, however, lies behind the guidance expert's psychological counseling and the psychotherapist's goal of self-acceptance. The existentialists deal with authenticity and value by demanding that we live our lives honestly, that we make our choices with as much consciousness as possible, that we be aware of the values that lie behind such choices, and that we not rationalize our way out of the consequences which ensue. In short, they make a plea for responsible decision-making.

A second area of convergence deals with the importance of irrational processes. The prominence of Freudian psychology on this issue is obvious and pre-eminent. What is not so obvious is that existential thought on unconscious processes actually preceded that of psychoanalysis in the writings of literary men such as Dostoevsky and Tolstoy and in the works of such philosophers as Nietzsche and Kierkegaard.[26] The contemporary existentialist concern for the non-rational in contrast to the unconscious is perhaps most obvious in the works of Camus,[27] who describes behavior which should be thought of not as a protest against reason, but as a protest against *mere* reason.

The concern for the irrational side of man in religion

is best seen in its realization that human existence is
impossible without some kind of faith. The religionist
has long recognized the necessity for commitment in order
to live, and that such commitment may not necessarily be
a rational or a conscious one. Note, for example, that the
commitment to rationality as a basis for living is not
necessarily a rational decision, nor is the commitment to
a non-rational basis for living necessarily an irrational decision. Thus, the shortcomings of *mere* rationality are
implicit in the religious concern for faith, and this concern represents an item of great wisdom which religion
shares with psychology and existentialism in their common pointing up of the irrational in man.

A third area of common concern is that of anxiety.
While it is true that the anxiety of the existentialists and
the religionists is more metaphysical than that of the psychologists, it is anxiety nevertheless. Both the religionists
and the existentialists speak of the anxiety which accompanies alienation—separation from fellow man, society,
and nature. While the religionists stress the anxiety which
accompanies separation from God, the existentialists
speak of the threat of non-being. At this point we see the
linkage with the more pedestrian anxiety of the psychologist. For the existentialist concept of non-being might be
physical death, and the immortality concern of religion
might be thought of as a psychological security measure;
or, non-being could be psychological death, or ego threat.
At this point note the tie-up to our earlier discussion of
authenticity. For if there is an imminent threat of non-
being, that is, of not becoming what one should become
in terms of one's individuality, then the threat to the
self is severe, and dread, or anxiety, is a natural consequence. One reason for the recent emergence of existential psychotherapy is the growing realization of a com-
monality between the existential anxiety of meaninglessness and the free-floating anxiety of the neurotic.

The final example of common concern is that of symbolic process. From the point of view of psychology, it
is unfortunately true that Jung has stood practically alone
in his prophetic writings on the importance of symbolic
manifestations for the understanding of both psychological and religious matters. The psychologists have branded

him as mystical and have essentially ignored him as un-scientific, whereas the religionists have not been too happy with his interpretation of concepts such as God in symbolic rather than literalistic terms. The discipline of religion has been reluctant to see the power and the deep insight of this view, although the recent indirect support from the writings of Cassirer, Langer, and other philosophers on symbolic forms has begun to have a very salutary impact on contemporary religious thought. This non-literalistic approach has been most potently stated by the Christian existential theologian Paul Tillich in his magnum opus, *Systematic Theology*. It is in this work that we see the complete integrative treatment—that is, in terms of psychology, existentialism, and re-ligion—of symbolism. For here we have the existential concern for the meaning which is invested in a religious symbol, the religious idolatry which is the lot of those who literalize such symbols, and the awareness that it is important not to speak psychological nonsense about such matters.

Now let us turn to several ideas which are central to existential thought and are fundamental to an eventual theory of man, which may be shared in part by one or both of the other two disciplines, but which are not clearly common to all three. I shall discuss the first two points together because they are interrelated. They are as follows: (1) existence is not essence and (2) man is not a machine. First, the existential view that existence is not essence. This view is essentially Lockean. It says that we all start life with nothing but the fact that we are here. We breathe, we eat, we grow, we make choices. Our lives are not determined or pre-determined by any pre-existing or abstract essences, values, or purposes. Contrary to Descartes, the existentialists say, "I am, therefore I think." In the process of existing and choosing we be-come some kind of essence which, however, still does not bind us. In short, man is free, and he makes him-self. Secondly, the existentialists say that man cannot be understood as a machine or robot. A given man at a given time does not know what he will do at the next moment, his essence is still evolving. Furthermore, he is not always rational, and in addition he does not follow

a certain set of rules or principles. In short, man is not
a thing, and therefore, scientific prediction regarding man
will not work. However, contemporary man is being
treated as if he were a thing, for he is being pushed
around by masses, big organizations, and urban industrialization. He is being compartmentalized by educational and occupational specialization. Finally he gets
to the point where he sees himself, not as a man, a
whole person with diversity of needs and purposes, but
only as a plumber, or a teacher, or a salesman. That is,
he sees himself functionally rather than as a human being. Such a dehumanized or fragmented man, treated
essentially as a thing, is existentially dead. Man in such
a state is not free; he is simply a robot. Existential man,
on the other hand, is free.

These two views are interrelated by the existential
assumption that man is free, not determined. Here is a
position diametrically opposed to that of scientific psychology. For psychology, in order to play the scientific
game, was forced to accept the assumption of determinism, and is proceeding as rapidly as possible with an
electronic brain as the current model for man. While
it must be admitted that psychology has learned much
about man on the basis of this assumption, it must also
be admitted that existentialism and religion have also
gained insights into man's nature by proceeding with the
opposite assumption. This raises the apparently unanswerable problem of free will versus determinism.[28] Let
us pause for a moderately lengthy discussion of this particular issue because of its very great importance for an
eventual theory of man. The assumption one makes regarding man's freedom is perhaps *the* important assumption regarding man's nature. For example, as a psychological scientist I operate within the philosophical framework of determinism. That is, I have faith that there is
order in human nature, just as the physical scientist has
faith that there is order in physical nature. The belief
in order implies that the identification of variables and
their interrelationships can be accomplished, and that
this procedure will lead to the specification of many "if-
then" relationships (see p. 49). The view of determinism
implies that *all* observable effects can be traced to some

specifiable prior agent or agents. In other words, all observable "thens" can be traced to a necessary and sufficient set of "ifs." "If" such and such conditions converge at a given point in space and time, "then" such and such events *must* occur at a later point in space and time. All this suggests that if scientists will continue to hack away diligently in their laboratories and studies they will eventually specify all the "if-then" relationships and a completely deterministic view of the universe will unfold before our eyes. The physicists of the 19th century, for example, felt so secure about their mechanical model of the physical universe that they were of the opinion that future developments in the area of physical sciences would consist merely of a mopping-up process involving little more than the computation of the next decimal point. Psychology, as a science of the behavior of organisms, is concerned with specifying the "if-then" relationships of the behavioral universe. Many of these relationships have been spelled out during the first half of the 20th century, and it begins to look as though man is going to be more successful in this endeavor than might be good for him. This concern has shown itself most pointedly in the fictitious efforts of Aldous Huxley in *Brave New World* and George Orwell in *1984*. In these novels "big brother" controls man's behavior to a considerable extent. If the assumption of determinism applies to human behavior as well as to the physical and biological universe, then knowledge of the relevant "if-then" relationships can lead to complete control over the behavior of men. This means that the awesome implications inherent in the books by Huxley and Orwell may be child's play in contrast to the "big brother" control which future dictators would be able to introduce. The psychological power of man over his fellow man is growing as the years go by. In view of what has been presented above, and in view of recent military technological developments in the area of nuclear energy, if psychological determinism is completely operative, I find myself forced to a logic of inevitability concerning the destruction of modern civilization.

While a thoroughgoing deterministic faith has paid

off handsomely in scientific thought to date, there have been certain 20th-century developments, namely the indeterminacy principle of Heisenberg, Einstein's position regarding relativity, the unpredictability of the single case, the operation of many variables, and the existence of a large segment of sheer ignorance, which indicate that a shift in the philosopher's orientation is in process. Let us suppose this is actually the case, namely that the physical universe and especially man's behavior is only deterministic in the sense of probability. That is, human behavior is orderly, but it is not completely deterministic. Does this lead us, then, to free choice? And how can we tie together the tendencies toward order and predictability with the tendencies toward chaos and unpredictability?

I shall throw out a simple hypothesis for consideration. It is this. *The greater the involvement of intelligence, the greater the freedom of choice*. This implies that the more intelligent organism is not as bound by his environment as the less intelligent organism, that the more intelligent organism is freer in the sense that he has a greater degree of choice. Let us take an obvious example in order to clarify the hypothesis. Contrast the adaptability of a moron with that of a genius. A moron might be considered lucky if he could follow the same simple path to work every day without getting lost from time to time. An Einstein, on the other hand, attempts to master the multifarious mazes of the entire physical universe. The degree of freedom open to an Einstein is infinitely greater than the possible choices which are available to a moron. Similarly, the emotionally confused individual becomes relatively rigid in his behavior patterns. In fact, the purpose of psychotherapy is to provide "insight," thereby restoring the effective intelligence of the individual. This process leads to a new sense of freedom, the possibility for a wider degree of choice in everyday living. Even more obvious is the contrast between inanimate and living objects. Inanimate objects possess no intelligence, and the degree of determinism which has been brought to bear on the physical universe is much greater than the degree of determinism which has been brought to bear on the biology and psychology of living things. Furthermore, it is clear that as we ascend the phyletic series in the animal kingdom, the presence of a larger and more complicated nervous system leads to greater and greater variability and flexibility in the adaptation of the organism to its environment. In other words, the degree of freedom in dealing with the environment increases as we move from amoeba to man. Effective intelligence, then, leads to more and more alternatives, and as this variability increases, it becomes more and more difficult to make exact predictions. Stated another way, the degree of determinism or predictability varies inversely with the degree of intelligence. It should be made clear that this conclusion does *not* lead to chaos; it leads to a probabilistic view of determinism as it relates to the behavior of man.

I would deny that this conclusion means that man has an *entirely* free will. While the writer cannot help but admire the existentialist position as it relates to self-determination and responsibility, the suggestion on the part of some critics that this means the existentialists ignore the findings of contemporary behavioral science is probably an erroneous interpretation of the existentialist position.[29] The point is that we do not have convincing evidence for either of the extreme positions—that man's behavior is completely free, or that it is completely determined. Is it not true that many aspects of man's behavior are, in fact, machine-like? And is it not equally true that such an approach is too reductive and will leave too much unaccounted for? Does this not suggest that psychology, for example, should become more humanistic, and at least go so far as to use the model of an organism rather than a machine? And isn't it also true that man as a completely free being is equally preposterous? Perhaps the dilemma of freedom versus determinism as far as man's behavior is concerned can best be resolved by discarding both of the extreme positions, which do not fit the full range of observation concerning man, in favor of the more realistic position of probabilistic determinism. This would mean that our behavior is variously determined or free, ranging from the complete determinism of a reflex action to the relatively free choice of what food a healthy man might eat at a cafeteria. The implication of this discussion is, of course, that the existentialists do not mean that man is *completely* free. What they do mean is that man is free in spite of the fact that he is hemmed in by circumstances, that man is he who is capable of knowingly making choices and accepting responsibility for them. The essential point the existentialist wants to make is that, however much I may attribute my actions to forces impinging on me, I know that I am not identical with the forces, but rather I am he who goes through my actions. Perhaps the strength of the existentialist position is their reminder that we are still men, and not things. Perhaps they feel it is necessary to swing the pendulum full course in the direction of freedom in the hope that contemporary man will at least move away from his present "scientized," "robotized" view of himself.

The final existential view which I want to call to your attention is the stress on the value and meaning of the immediately apprehendable aesthetic experience. This is one of the positive by-products of their protest against "mere" reason, and a further reminder of the artistic aspect of man's nature. It is related to their stress on living in the moment, maximizing one's awareness, existing fully. This view overlaps Zen and other Eastern philosophic and religious views, and it is consistent with Northrop's[30] plea that Western man needs to balance his identification with the rational or theoretical approach to life by the Eastern concern for the aesthetic. While it is doubtful that psychology has any objection at this point, it is also true that as a discipline it has had little to say on this issue. Perhaps the only systematic exposition within psychology which has stressed the aesthetic or intuitive component is that of Jung, whose fourfold typology requires that a healthy psyche balance the rational and the intuitive along with the sensory and the feeling functions. Perhaps the main point to be made here is that Western culture, including Western therapeutic practice, could profit greatly by openness to the ancient therapeutic practices of Eastern culture. Close examination of such procedures would certainly result in confirmation of much that is being done today in psychotherapy as well as point the way to new insights which could be applied to currently over-rational, aesthetically deprived Western man. Such an approach might even lead to a broader view of the role of the therapist; namely, as more of a sage and guide. He might be seen more as the archetypal "wise old man" rather than the more restrictive "adjustor-to-society" or medieval-prototype mind healer, which is currently the case.

Jung, while not an existentialist, is also much concerned about the nature of man. While he places much more stress on non-rational and non-conscious processes, he deals with the problem of self-realization under the rubric of individuation. Jung's systematic position and therapeutic procedure is probably more religiously oriented than that of any other leading contemporary psychoanalyst. It is probable that this is the reason he has been listened to more by experts in religion and literature than by the scientific experts. I suspect that the behavioral scientists are correct in not listening to him as a scientist, but that they are wrong in failing to listen to him as the archetypal "wise old man." One expert who has listened to Jung is the historian Arnold Toynbee. Whether, from your perspective, he listened rightly or wrongly, many of Toynbee's views concerning the rise and fall of civilizations are based upon Jungian conceptions of the nature of man. This includes such ideas as the importance of the myth in the development of the *Weltanschauung*, the stress he places on unconscious processes, and the importance attached to the emergence of symbols in the control of social and political events. There is also a strong Jungian influence evident in Toynbee's position on progress, which he claims depends upon the extent to which a civilization manifests spiritual or religious concerns.[31] In his concept of "challenge and response" Toynbee indicates that, in a series of challenges to the continuance of a civilization, if the response does not finally become a religious one, the civilization will probably decline. What is of particular concern to us at this point is the stress which Toynbee places on individual personality and creativity in meeting the challenge of continued existence. Here we see an amazing convergence of thinking on the problem of existence at the individual level as discussed by existentialist philosophers, psychologists, and theologians, and at the civilization level as discussed by an historian. A deep concern for values and a consequent release of creative energy is common to both of these approaches.

Thus we see that a philosophy and a psychology of being lie at the center of the network of meaning, value, and personality. As we exist we become aware of values, and we grow into these essences or patterns. We choose, we behave, and we "become"; and we choose and become in terms of what we value most. And as we live out our lives in terms of a wide variety of value schemes, probably primarily unconsciously "chosen," we are living out an underlying philosophy of what each of us believes is the essence of being, and since we each possess a unique psychology, the answers differ somewhat both on an individual level and on a cultural level.[32] Each of us as an individual, and as a member of a society, has deep concerns about his personal and group being, and how he can best relate this way of being to other peoples, to the physical world about us, and eventually, to the cosmos. As we reach out to this larger environment of others and the cosmos, we extend our personalities beyond a purely self-orientation in search of wholeness. It is at this point that man's concern for value and meaning merges into the religious quest, for it is the religious sentiment in man which reaches out for an all-inclusive *Weltanschauung* and a fullness of being. It would appear to be obvious that such seeking is a lifetime quest. That is, as long as one exists one must be concerned with the problem of what it means to be, and in concerning one's self with what it means to be in the fullest and most significant manner, one eventually gets pushed to one's ultimate values, one's world-view. And as soon as we stop doubting or questioning, as soon as we come to the conclusion that we finally have the answers, we have, in the psychological, philosophical, and religious sense, ceased to be.

At this point we come to an interesting and unexpected tie-up to the major thesis of this book. We have been primarily concerned with the dangers of encapsulation. Nowhere is this danger more potent than in the area of religion. For there is no more pathetic, constricted, meaningless, and irreligious individual than the encapsulated religionist. We are suggesting that the religious sentiment described above requires a breadth and depth of concern and awareness which the encapsulated religious man does not have. We are also saying that the truly unencapsulated man is a deeply religious man. That is, he is religious in the broad sense in which we are using the term, implying the search for ultimate values, meaning, and wholeness in life. Such a view of religion could not require rigid adherence to a dogma or creed, nor could it adhere to a religious sect which proclaims all the answers for all of time and space. It could not tolerate "specialism" [33] in religion any more than the unencapsulated man can tolerate "specialism" in living. The unencapsulated religious man requires that we break through the barriers of looking at religion partially and substitute a more complete look before making pronouncements concerning religious truth.

If we could engender a more open approach to religion, I believe that a transformation in the religious life of man would occur. One of the most important manifestations of this transformation would become evident in our awareness of the symbol and the myth as conveyors of (religious) truth. A more complete acquaintance with the major religions of the world would point to the underlying similarities as well as differences of the major religions. The existence of several Messiahs, several bibles, and several views of God would force us to reconsider the dangers of literalism in interpreting religious writings and lead us to a deeper awareness of the essentially symbolic nature of religion. I shall deal more fully with this point in the next chapter.

NOTES

1. G. W. Allport, P. E. Vernon, and G. Lindzey, A Study of Values, Revised Edition, New York: Houghton, Mifflin Co., 1951.

2. Data provided by Dr. F. A. Kingsbury, private communication. Similar data are available in the test manual of the Allport-Vernon-Lindzey Study of Values cited above.

3. J. S. Bruner and C. G. Goodman, Value and need as organizing factors in perception, J. Abn. & Soc. Psychol., 1947, 42, 33-44.

4. J. S. Bruner, W. Postman, and E. McGinnies, Personal values as selective factors in perception, *J. Abn. & Soc. Psychol.*, 1948, *43*, 142-154.

5. A preliminary version of an inventory, *The Psycho-Epistemological Profile*, has been constructed and administered to contrasting groups such as scientists, artists, mathematicians, and literature students. Out of nine mathematicians, for example, the rational approach was ranked first, with either empiricism or intuitionism second, and authoritarianism last. In the case of the tenth mathematician his profile had intuitionism first with rationalism second, then empiricism and authoritarianism. A second pilot study involved administering the Profile to 10 mathematicians, 13 biologists, and 12 advanced students in the fine arts. The group results came out as expected, with the mathematicians ranking rationalism at the apex of their hierarchy, the biologists ranking empiricism highest, and the fine arts students ranking intuition highest. A revised experimental form of the inventory is now available for research purposes.

6. In W. Somerset Maugham, *Tellers of Tales*, New York: Doubleday, Doran & Co., 1939.

7. Anton Chekhov, "The Cherry Orchard," in *Plays by Anton Chekhov*, London: Duckworth, 1920.

8. Leo Tolstoy, *The Death of Ivan Ilytch*, translated by Aylmer Maude, Oxford: Oxford University Press. In W. Somerset Maugham, *op. cit.*, pp. 589-590.

9. *Ibid*, p. 590.

10. J. P. Marquand, *Point of No Return*, Boston: Little, Brown, 1949.

11. J. Phillips, *The Second Happiest Day*, New York: Bantam Books, 1953.

12. Sloane Wilson, *The Man in the Grey Flannel Suit*, New York: Simon & Schuster, 1955.

13. Arthur Miller, *The Death of a Salesman*, New York: Bantam Books, 1951.

14. A great deal has been written on this topic in the United States in recent years, especially since Sputnik. For my views see J. R. Royce, Adjustment versus intellectual achievement, *Improving College and University Teaching*, 1960, *8*, 45-48.

15. See the recent book edited by Rollo May, E. Angel, and H. Ellenberger, *Existence: A New Dimension in Psychiatry and Psychology*, New York: Basic Books, 1959, and Viktor Frankl, *The Doctor and the Soul*, New York: Alfred A. Knopf, 1953.

16. Werner Wolff, *Values and Personality*, New York: Grune and Stratton, 1950, p. 53.

17. Paul Tillich, *The Courage to Be*, New Heaven: Yale University Press, 1952.

18. G. W. Allport, *Becoming*, New Haven: Yale University Press, 1955.

19. *Ibid.*, p. 95.

20. See also Allport's book on *The Individual and His Religion*, New York: Macmillan, 1950.

21. W. H. Clark, *The Psychology of Religion*, New York: Macmillan Co., 1958.

22. P. Johnson, *Psychology of Religion*, Revised Edition, Nashville: Abingdon Press, 1959.

23. O. H. Mowrer, *The Crisis in Psychiatry and Religion*, New York: D. Van Nostrand Company, Inc., 1961.

24. A. H. Maslow, *Toward a Psychology of Being*, New York: D. Van Nostrand Company, Inc., 1962.

25. See, for example, the journal *Pastoral Psychology*. See also the newly established journals such as *J. of Humanistic Psychology, J. of Existential Psychiatry*, and *Review of Existential Psychology and Psychiatry*, which, while not specifically devoted to relating psychology to religion, represent a response to the contemporary impact of existentialist thinking, and which will, in my opinion, form the basis for building a bridge between the two disciplines.

26. See Walter Kaufman, *Existentialism From Dostoevski to Sartre*, New York: Meridian Books, 1957, and William Barrett, *Irrational Man*, New York: Doubleday & Co., 1958.

27. A. Camus, *The Stranger*, New York: Alfred A. Knopf, 1957; A. Camus, *The Myth of Sisyphus*, New York: Alfred A. Knopf, 1955; F. S. C. Northrop, *op. cit.*, and *The Meeting of East and West*, New York: Macmillan, 1946.

28. In the discussion which follows the writer makes no claim to philosophic sophistication in dealing with the hoary issue of free will versus determinism. I did not feel it was either necessary or appropriate to probe this issue in depth in the present context, particularly in view of the fact that it appears to be unresolvable. One working solution to this dilemma is to accept the position of determinism when working and thinking as a scientist and to accept the position of freedom when functioning as an individual human being. While this does not solve the issue, it at least accepts the paradoxical legitimacy of both positions.

29. It seems appropriate to mention, in passing, an obvious contrast between existential and behavioristic psychology at this juncture. Behavioristic psychology, whether or not the behavioristic psychologist is aware of it, tends to say that a man is identical with the forces impinging on him. The ultra-environ-

mentalistic, ultra-deterministic position of the classical behavior-
ist, a view not unknown among neo-behaviorists, reaches its
zenith in the writings of John B. Watson. He epitomized this
approach when he wrote that he could take any normal infant
"and train him to become any type of specialist I might select
—doctor, lawyer, artist, merchant-chief, and yes, even beggar-
man and thief. . . ." (In J. B. Watson, *Behaviorism*, New
York: W. W. Norton and Co., 1925, p. 82.) One reason
existential psychology is having a stronger impact on contemporary thought in psychology than might have been predicted as
little as ten years ago is that ultra-behaviorism renders bankrupt
the psychologist who insists on dealing with man in his fullest
stature intellectually, conceptually, and practically (e.g., the
field of clinical psychology).

30. F. S. C. Northrop, *op. cit.*

31. For a more complete development of this point see
M. Hunnex, *"Toynbee's idea of etherialization as a criterion of
progress."* Unpublished doctoral dissertation, University of Redlands, California, 1957.

32. For example, see Ruth Benedict, *op. cit.*

33. This does not deny the point that religious involvement
always implies commitment. The suggestion being made here is
that the religious involvement of the unencapsulated man is
accompanied by more awareness and openness than the religious
commitment of the encapsulated man.

8

Symbol, Myth, and Reality

> *"It is not given to us to grasp the truth, which is identical with the divine, directly. We perceive it only in reflection, in example and symbol, in singular and related appearances. It meets us as a kind of life which is incomprehensible to us, and yet we cannot free ourselves from the desire to comprehend it."*
>
> —GOETHE

> *". . . the myth is the combination of symbols of our ultimate concern."*
>
> —PAUL TILLICH

SIGN AND SYMBOL

In answer to the query "What is man?" several contemporary thinkers have suggested that the orthodox definition of man as a "rational animal" needs to be replaced by defining him as a "symbolizing animal." Suzanne Langer, for example, says: "Not higher sensitivity, not longer memory or even quicker association sets man so far above other animals that he can regard them as denizens of a lower world; no, it is the power of using symbols that makes him lord of the earth." [1] Leslie White, an anthropologist, points out that "There is a *fundamental* difference between the mind of man and the mind of nonman. This difference is one of kind, not one of degree. And the gap between the two types is of greatest importance—at least to the science of comparative behavior. Man uses symbols; no other creature does. A creature either uses symbols or he does not; there are no intermediate stages." [2] Cassirer takes us a few steps further when he points out that "Man [is] . . . no longer in a physical universe, man lives in a symbolic universe. Language, myth, art, and religion are parts of this universe. They are the varied threads which weave the symbolic net. . . . That symbolic thought and symbolic

129

behavior are among the most characteristic features of human life, and that the whole progress of human culture is based on these conditions, is undeniable." [3]

The symbol, then, is the key to human behavior and the development of what is known as civilization. The ability of man to invoke the symbolization process is what differentiates him from the other animal forms. Animal psychologists have clearly demonstrated that the previously held distinction of rationality simply is not true. The problem-solving ability of sub-human primates, as demonstrated in the researches which emanate from such centers as Dr. Harry Harlow's[4] Primate Laboratory at the University of Wisconsin and the Yerkes Laboratories of Primate Psychobiology,[5] is quite advanced. They are quite capable, for example, of categorizing, that is, of performing a type of simple taxonomic classification of a variety of objects. The performance of the rhesus monkey in the manipulation of a series of rakes as simulated "tools" would rarely be surpassed by human infants of comparable age. In this connection, several psychologists[6] have actually reared chimpanzees along with their own children (and I might add, with apparently no evil effects on the child, although the effect on the chimp is unknown) and have demonstrated that the chimp actually surpasses the human child at certain ages and in some types of mental ability. Of course the chimp has a much shorter life span than the human, and when one corrects for maturity level rather than comparing on the basis of absolute age, the child is superior to the chimp. Estimates have been made, however, that certain individual sub-human primates can perform at a human mental age level of around six or seven. While sub-human problem solving is most convincingly demonstrable at the primate level, there is also evidence that animals much lower in the animal kingdom exhibit the ability to reason. Numerous experiments have shown this in the dog[7] and the cat, and N. R. F. Maier[8] has even shown it to be true of the rat! It may be true that even lower animal forms are capable of thought but, to my knowledge, it has not been convincingly demonstrated in the laboratory.

While rats and monkeys may think, and parrots talk, and the birds and bees communicate, and the ants live according to a highly structured communistic society, no animal species has developed the symbolic form as has man. The most intelligent monkey or baboon has not yet developed a calculus, or written a sonata, or demonstrated a religious concern. In short, lower animal forms are clearly highly adaptable and intelligent organisms, but they have not developed the symbolic forms typical of human culture.

For one thing, they have not developed the most elementary symbolic form—language. While it is true that a dog may be conditioned to respond to a certain verbal command, it is not true that dogs, or other subhuman forms, comprehend words in the abstract sense, and it certainly is obvious that the species "canine" has not developed a dog language which is passed on from one generation of pups to the next as a part of canine culture. The emergence of symbolic or meaningful language as opposed to sign language is dramatically illustrated in the following passage from the story of Helen Keller,[9] a blind deaf-mute.

This morning, while she was washing, she wanted to know the name for "water." When she wants to know the name of anything, she points to it and pats my hand. I spelled w-a-t-e-r and thought no more about it until after breakfast . . . we went out to the pump house, and I made Helen hold her mug under the spout while I pumped. As the cold water gushed forth, filling the mug, I spelled w-a-t-e-r in Helen's free hand. The word coming so close upon the sensation of cold water rushing over her hand seemed to startle her. She dropped the mug and stood as one transfixed. A new light came into her face. She spelled "water" several times. Then she dropped on the ground and asked for its name and pointed to the pump and the trellis and suddenly turning round she asked for my name. I spelled "teacher." All the way back to the house she was highly excited, and learned the name of every object she touched, so that in a few hours she had added thirty new words to her vocabulary. The next morning she got up like a radiant fairy. She has flitted from object to object, asking the name of everything. . . . Everything must have a name now. Wherever we go, she asks eagerly for the names of things she has not learned at home. She is anxious for her friends to spell, and eager to teach the letters to everyone she meets. She drops the signs and pantomime she used before, as soon as she has words to supply their place, and the acquirement of a new word affords her the liveliest pleasure. And we notice that her face grows more expressive each day.[10]

It is true, of course, that lower animals may go through an experience such as that described above and that we have merely failed to understand the language of lower animals. Be that as it may, archaeologists and anthropologists have failed to unearth cultural artifacts which would tend to support such a notion, and we are forced to remain with our original contention. Perhaps the observation most relevant to this discussion is to be found in a study by Wolfe.[11] In this study Wolfe showed that chimpanzees learned to use different colored poker chips in order to acquire a variety of food rewards. If the chimp, for example, preferred a banana, he would cash in five blue chips for one red one, slide it into the banana-dispensing machine, and get his reward. In other words, up to a point, we can say that Wolfe's chimps placed values on tokens, in much the same manner as the human evaluates quarters and dimes in making a variety of purchases. Wolfe and other psychologists claim that this type of experiment constitutes proof for the involvement of symbolic processes in the sub-human primate. The case history of Helen Keller suggests that the key to the humanizing process—for that is what Helen Keller was undergoing—lies in the development of speech. When Miss Keller could name things, she became delirious in her awareness of what it means to communicate intelligently. And then she did what apparently the ape does not do: "she drops the signs and pantomime she used before, as soon as she has words to supply their place. . . ."[12]

Meaning for the lower animal, then, can only be communicated in terms of signs, whereas the human can communicate with both signs and symbols. Let me pursue this distinction between sign and symbol and animal and man a little further. While it is true that the sign and the symbol are alike in that they both point beyond themselves to "something else," it is also true that the "something else" they point to is quite different. The "something else" which the sign "points to" or "stands for" is quite definite and specific. But while the "something else" which the symbol "points to" or "stands for" is also definite and specific, it can "stand for" a wide variety of things at different times and places. Stated in a more general way, the sign provides us with a one-to-one relationship, whereas the symbol provides us with a one-to-many relationship.

The one-to-one relationship of the sign is nicely exemplified in the case of the conditioned response, which can be illustrated as in Figure 12. The usual response to

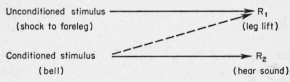

Fig. 12. An example of avoidance conditioning

an electric shock to the foreleg is to lift the leg so as to avoid the shock (hence the name for this type of conditioned response, avoidance conditioning). The usual response to the sound of a bell is to simply hear the sound. The unusual connection between the bell (the C.S.) and the response of lifting the leg (R_1) is the conditioned response. This is an unusual response in the sense that an animal, say a dog, does not ordinarily lift his foreleg upon hearing the sound of a bell. However, because of the reinforcement of electric shock, because of the constant pairing of bell and shock, the result is the elicitation of a leg lift whenever the bell is sounded. In other words, the bell is now a "sign" of the shock. It signifies something very specific and definite, and further, it signifies one, and only one, thing. It is a "sign" which reveals a one-to-one relationship, that is, bell "means" shock.

The one-to-many relationship of the symbol,[13] on the other hand, can be seen in a fairly typical example of a dream symbol. If three different people dream about a house, it can mean three different things. In one case it might represent the wish-fulfillment of a tenant farmer whose life-time goal is to own his own home. In the second case it might represent a man's fear of being "closed in" by fateful circumstances. And in the third case it might represent the Freudian notion of female sexuality. Here we note that the symbol "house" "points to" or "stands for" something else which is definite and specific, but it represents a different thing for each of the three dreamers. In other words, the symbol, allowing for a variety of interpretations as to what is meant, provides us with a one-to-many relationship. The symbol remains the same, but its meaning varies with the percipient and circumstance. A rich symbol, a symbol of depth, is a rich, deep symbol by virtue of the surplus meaning. This will be seen very clearly if I elaborate on a rich symbol such as the bullfight so that we may see the variety of meanings which it can evoke.

White defines a symbol as "a thing the value or meaning of which is bestowed upon it by those who use it. I say 'thing' because a symbol may have any kind of physical form; it may have the form of a material object, a color, a sound, an odor, a motion of an object, a taste." [14] And I have defined the symbol as a "thing" which represents something else in a one-to-many relationship. If we take the bullfight as a sign rather than a symbol, we should have to interpret it literally somehow. We should have to conclude ridiculous things such as that the purpose of the fiesta is to kill the bull, or that the bullfighter is a butcher. As an aficionado of the bullfight I assert that it is not a literalistic "thing," but rather, that it is symbolic. Symbolic of what? For me it is so pregnant with meaning that it is capable of serving as a representation of life itself, in the same sense as the drama or a novel. For the bullfight involves life and death, courage and cowardice, gaiety and sadness. The good bullfighter represents the heroic quality in man.[15] He stands quietly and bravely in the middle of an arena with nothing but a red piece of cloth in his hand as a thousand pounds of death comes charging at him. The people in the audience know that in a similar situation they would run. They recognize bravery, the courage to face death, which is necessary if one is to be a matador.

The idolization of such courage is so great in Latin countries that when the great Manolete was killed in the bullring in 1947 Spain went into a state of national mourning! And here, among other things, we see why it was said earlier that the bullfight is a miniature of life. Death is a part of life, and it is an integral part of the bullfight. As in life, death hovers; it is inevitable, if not for the man, certainly for the bull. And in life, each of us must eventually die. One of the things the matador is saying when he fights bravely is that the way we die is important, or, that what is really important is how we live. That is, cowardice does not befit the matador.

In many ways the famous Mexican matador Procuna is the best symbol of man to emerge from the annals of tauromachy. Procuna has exhibited outstanding courage and cowardice in the arena, as does "everyman" in the arena of life. Procuna has been known to exhibit his fear quite openly and unashamedly. He is superstitious, and when he gets the idea that "the bull is on to him," he will not fight him. He simply goes through some "safe" motions, elicits too much help from his cuadrilla,[16] and may leap the barrera[17] repeatedly. Such "cowardly" behavior is booed with gusto by the audience. Psychologically, it represents disapproval for the "weak" side of man. Such behavior is all right for the ordinary man, but not for a matador.[18] On the other hand, Procuna's status as a great matador arises out of the absolute control and complete courage which he exhibits on other occasions. This ambivalence of Procuna's, this very human characteristic of a man from whom the crowd demands a superhuman performance, is why I regard him as an excellent symbol of "everyman." One difference between the bullfighter and the rest of us is that the bullfighter's lack of courage is evident for all to see, whereas the ordinary man can hide such human failings in the dark recesses of his private memory.

The bullfight is also a very gay fiesta. The opening music is stirring, the clothing worn by the participants is very colorful, and the crowd is in a holiday mood. The anticipation before the start of the corrida[19] is so great that the crowd cheers uncontrollably when the first few notes of the trumpet announce that the time has come to start the fight. As the toreros[20] parade into the arena, great roars of approval greet their ears. They parade with beauty and grace across the arena. The beginning of a bullfight points up another aspect of this unusually deep symbol—its ritualistic nature. Each bullfight lasts 20 minutes. It always begins with music, followed by the parade. Each fight consists of three parts with subparts within each of the three major "acts." The bullfight is highly structured, it is highly ritualistic, and, for some, it is even religious in its manner and message. In fact, the early history of bullfighting is tied in rather directly with religious ritual. The bull itself is a well known religious symbol in many cultures. And the sun, another well known religious symbol, is also an important aspect of the bullfight.

The bullfight, then, is many things, and to a native of a Latin land, it may well represent the epitome of all that is good and worthwhile in the world. On the other hand, to an unsophisticated or uninformed American it might represent simple-minded sadism, or a "primitive" custom of a backward people. Perhaps the major point to be made is that the meaning which a symbol conveys depends primarily on the conveyor and the context. The symbol in and of itself remains the same, but the interpretations attached to it are many and varied. In one sense this richness of the depth symbol is very helpful and useful to man, but from the point of view of establishing truth, the surplus meaning of symbols is a very difficult problem to deal with.

The examples of the bullfight and of Helen Keller suggest that the symbol is essentially a way of coming to grips with the environment, perhaps literally coming to terms with life. For in each case we are concerned with the reactions of an individual to an experience. Something significant happens to a person (perhaps the only true reality is the experience itself), and the person feels the need to conceptualize this experience and perhaps to try to communicate something of what he thought or felt to others. We call this process of conceptualizing and communicating symbolization. In the case of Helen Keller it is particularly powerful because of the obvious way it releases thought. Before the process of naming came to her, Helen Keller's approach to the environment was essentially mechanical. But after language became a part of her repertoire, the whole world of thought opened up before her. She was now equipped with an open-ended weapon in adapting to life. Whereas previously she was highly stimulus bound, now she could transcend the stimulus input because her cortex was to become a more active part of her psychobiological machinery. As Langer puts it, "symbolization is the starting point of all human intellection." [21] In other words, symbolic forms, such as language, myth, art, and religion, are not mere fanciful expressions of emotional needs, but contain within them a plethora of meanings and concepts which are worthy of our serious consideration. It is probable, of course, that such symbolic forms are more difficult to come to grips with than are literalistic signs, but surely it is folly to turn our backs on insightful approaches to reality simply because of the difficulties of complexity and obscurity. An excellent example of the complexity and obscurity on the one hand and the valuable insight on the other hand, which is typical of symbolic expression, is the case of dream material. Does it fit Langer's suggestion that symbolization is the starting point of all human intellection? Or does it come closer to the Freudian notion of pure and simple wish-fulfillment? As is so often the case in opposing positions, there seems to be some truth in each view.

The psychologist Calvin S. Hall has conducted one of the few empirical studies in this area. In a recent book, which is based on an analysis of 10,000 dreams, he says that "the language of a dream consists of pictures which are the concrete perceptible representations of a mind's ideas. . . . We study dreams in order to find out what people are thinking about during sleep." [22] In other words, he offers us a cognitive theory of dreams, suggesting that dreaming is an analogical type of thinking quite comparable to other types of analogical thinking, but that we are merely less conscious of ourselves and of the material with which we are dealing. Whereas in a waking state a man may demand that his thinking be cast within a certain space-time framework, in his dreams this same man may float in and out of space and time quite

illogically. Psychoanalysts are quick to point out that the
usual logical requirements are completely inappropriate
in trying to interpret dreams, that psychological requirements are much more relevant. Any attempt to interpret
dream material as a sign language is doomed to failure,
for such manifestations are by definition a part of the
symbolic universe and must, therefore, be analyzed on
their own terms. Dream books and Freudian sexual re-
ductionism commit this error and have thereby been
led into a blind alley. The contemporary psychoanalytic
approach to dream analysis is summarized by Ruth Monroe[23] as follows:

(1) The underlying trend is discernible through many
types of material, derived from different sources.

(2) The underlying unconscious trend observed has
internal consistency, as regards both content and type
of "thinking."

(3) It is consistent with what is already known about
the patient in analysis.

(4) It leads readily to fruitful elaboration along the
lines consonant with the gradually emerging understanding of the patient.

All four of these criteria have to do with consistency
in one way or another, the first one imposing an external
consistency, the second one requiring internal consistency, the third one involving what might be called tem-
poral consistency, and the last one requiring what I will
label theoretical consistency. All four of these criteria
also imply that the analyst must be alert for the functional significance of the dream. For, as was stated earlier, symbolizing is a way of adapting to the environment.
This is true whether the symbolic manifestation be in
the form of a dream, humor, a myth, the usual artistic
and literary expressions, religious and political symbols,
expressive movements, or neurotic and psychotic symptoms. Much of symbolization occurs at an unconscious
level, particularly if it ties in closely with personal adjustment problems. For it is at this point that the well
known mechanisms such as rationalization, regression,
repression, and compensation come into the picture. One
of these unconscious mechanisms is particularly germane
to this discussion, namely that of symbolism. This phe-

nomenon is very nicely exemplified by the case of Lady
Macbeth. You will recall that Lady Macbeth is a som-
nambulist, and that she washes her hands as she paces,
saying repeatedly in her sleep, "Out, damned spot! out,
I say!" The unconscious handwashing is *as if* she could,
in fact, wash the blood from her hands, thereby remov-
ing the guilt for her misdeed. This particular example
is a clear case of the workings of unconscious processes.
Other examples have been given which just as obviously
involve conscious processes. The extent to which conscious or unconscious processes are involved in any specific symbolic manifestation can be readily determined
in many cases, but is a debatable question in most instances. For example, to what extent are unconscious
processes involved in something so apparently conscious
as composing a symphony or writing a novel? And to
what extent are conscious processes involved when men's
thoughts are "guided" by such symbols as the swastika,
the hammer and sickle, or the stars and stripes?

THE VIEWS OF JUNG, CASSIRER, AND TILLICH [24]

Jung takes the position that unconscious processes are
extremely important in symbolization, particularly as they
relate to personal adustment and the psychological meaning of the myth. As it relates to personal adjustment,
for example, he points out that a dream series indicates
not only information concerning the individual's past
experiences, but that it points to the future as well. That
is, dream contents are goal oriented in terms of the development of the person, and important clues concerning
the process of individuation[25] lie within such contents.
There is no implication that one can predict the future,
but rather, that dream contents represent interpretable
and valuable symbolic information concerning the psyche.
By tapping the unconscious one may be able, for example,
to identify those highly emotionally toned phenomena
known as complexes. And if properly tuned in, an analyst
has invaluable clues concerning the client's need for ego
support, fantasy expression, or release from his depend-
ence on the psychiatric situation. Frequently the initial
dream serves as a useful statement of the problem itself,

plus providing a prognosis concerning the outcome. Recurrent dreams suggest a character problem. And "big dreams," dreams containing archetypal material such as the mandala symbol, frequently forecast a significant step toward individuation. The major point here is that the unconscious is more likely to come up with a solution to a deep adjustment problem than are our conscious processes. This view is widely held in certain primitive cultures where "big dreams" are regarded as common property and are told to the entire tribe. There is, in fact, a Malayan society, the Senoi, where people are told to go back and re-dream until a resolution occurs. It is obvious that they have great respect for the dream as a purposeful effort to solve a problem. Further, the functional significance of a dream lies in the fact that it is primarily concerned with presenting new material to the ego for assimilation. As resistance lowers, more and more dream material will be admissible to consciousness, with the consequent increase in self awareness. And with the increase in self awareness, new strength emerges.

Psychotherapists of a wide variety of persuasions are agreed upon one thing if nothing else, namely, the presence of untapped inner resources lying deep within the psyche, presumably surging upward from the unconscious level. Carl Rogers speaks of this as a natural growth process, Jung calls it individuation, and Maslow calls it self-actualization. There is good evidence for this, and what is more, there are a variety of indications which suggest that our inner resources, or our unconscious resources, are essentially untapped. Our ignorance concerning unconscious processes is so profound that J. G. Miller has been able to seriously discuss 16 different meanings of the term in a 329-page book on the subject.[26] Here is a door we have barely opened, and while its rooms are essentially unknown, we can be certain it leads to a house of many mansions.

Jung's position is typically psychoanalytic at the level of the "personal unconscious" and the usual dream symbolism which emanates therefrom. But he adds another level of unconsciousness, commonly known as the collective unconscious, but more adequately described as the objective unconscious. In this concept the term "collective" means that portion of the unconscious which is common to all men, that is, the opposite of personal and subjective—hence the term "collective" or "objective." And by the term "unconscious" he means the "non-differentiated creativity of which man is not aware." The symbolic manifestations which emanate from the collective unconscious Jung calls archetypes.[27] They represent the recurrent themes or ideas of mankind, regardless of time or space. The great mother, the old wise man, the eternal wonder child, and the hero are examples of Jungian archetypes. Jung claims that these major themes transcend time and space, that they have done so in the past, and that they will emerge again in the future. Where does he get his evidence for such statements? He objects to the charge of mysticism and claims two types of empirical evidence: one, from case histories, especially dream contents, and two, from detailed analysis of the myths of the world. In answer to the charge that he is forcing "mystical" concepts on his data by selection, etc., he invites others to make similar analyses for themselves so that they might see that the concepts were forced upon him from the data, rather than vice versa. His data from both sources are voluminous, the clinical data having been compiled from his own practice as an analytical psychologist, and the mythological data having been compiled over a period of some 50 years of ethnological investigation. He has made field observations among the American Indians in Arizona and tribes in Africa, and he has collected and analyzed myths from a large sampling of the major civilizations and religions of the world.[28]

Jung's claim highlights the problem of how to interpret the symbol and myth. For while he is lambasted for providing weak data and labeled "mystic" by the scientist, he is simultaneously lauded for his empirical data and labeled "insightful" by the humanist. Can he be both sage and fool in one breath? Does he provide us with knowledge or not? If so, what are its limitations? Perhaps it would be correct to say that he meets the criteria for "symbolic" or "humanistic" knowledge, but fails to meet the criteria for "sign" or "scientific" knowledge. It will be necessary for us to clarify what we mean by "symbolic" knowledge before we proceed further with this issue.

Because of the greater ambiguity which surrounds symbolic validity, the theologian Paul Tillich feels that it is an error to speak of the truth or falsehood of a symbol in a purely cognitive sense. Such a judgement would reduce the symbol to a sign. Rather Tillich[29] elaborates on the following six characteristics of the symbol: (1) it points beyond itself to something else, (2) it participates in that to which it points, (3) it opens up levels of reality which are otherwise closed, (4) it unlocks hitherto unknown dimensions and elements of the psyche, (5) it cannot be produced intentionally, and (6) symbols are not made; they grow and die. On the last two characteristics, for example, Tillich makes the point that "symbols of faith cannot be replaced by other symbols, such as artistic ones, and they cannot be removed by scientific criticism. They have a genuine standing in the human mind, just as science and art have. Their symbolic character is their truth and their power. Nothing less than symbols and myths can express our ultimate concern.[30] Thus, in his elaboration of the validity of the religious symbol, rather than speak of its truth criteria, he speaks of it as being authentic as opposed to inauthentic, adequate as opposed to inadequate, and divine as opposed to demonic.[31] Religiously speaking, a symbol is authentic as opposed to inauthentic if it leads to a genuine encounter with ultimate reality, symbols are adequate if the ultimate is revealed through the finite medium, and symbols are divine rather than demonic only if our concerns are raised beyond the preliminary and the idolatrous. The literalistic distortion of a myth would be an example of an inadequate symbol, and a religious commitment to a political ideal, such as was frequently done by Hitler's followers, is an example of a demonic symbolic involvement.

If it is misleading to equate symbolic validity with cognitive truth, on what grounds can we accept whatever it is that symbols have to offer us? The answer seems to be on symbolic grounds, on the territory wherein the symbol has its strength—in short, in its ability to open up new dimensions of reality. Herein lies the validity of a living symbol, for it makes us aware in ways which simply cannot occur at the purely sign level. For, of the two, it is only the symbol which participates in the reality to which it points. In this sense the living symbol is indispensable, whereas the sign can be replaced with another sign.

> All arts create symbols for a level of reality which cannot be reached in any other way. A picture and a poem reveal elements of reality which cannot be approached scientifically. In the creative work of art we encounter reality in a dimension which is closed for us without such works. The symbol . . . not only opens up dimensions and reality which otherwise would remain unapproachable but also unlocks dimensions and elements of our soul. . . . A great play gives us not only a new vision of the human scene, but it opens up hidden depths of our being. Thus we are able to receive what the play reveals to us in reality. There are within us dimensions of which we cannot become aware except through symbols. . . .[32]

The opening up of otherwise unavailable insights to reality is the key to the knowledge-giving quality of the symbol. This depth quality of the symbol is also the essence of the view of the philosopher Ernst Cassirer, perhaps the outstanding contemporary thinker on the epistemology of the symbol. Cassirer develops the thesis that all knowledge, including science, is symbolic. He sees the various major cultural achievements, such as language, art, religion, and science, as varieties of symbolic forms—creations which emanate from the mind of men. His point is that raw sensory inputs do not emerge from man's brain unchanged. Upon reaching the cortical level, the raw inputs of the mind of man are transformed into one or another symbolic manifestation. And whether it be science or music, dream or myth, the dance or fantasy, it represents the effort of man's mind to formulate an interpretation of reality. In his *Language and Myth*, Cassirer spells out this symbolization process when he says:

> . . . myth, art, language and science appear as symbols; not in the sense of mere figures which refer to some given reality by means of suggestion and allegorical renderings, but in the sense of forces each of which produces and posits a

world of its own. . . . Thus the special symbolic forms are not imitations, but *organs* of reality, since it is solely by their agency that anything real becomes an object for intellectual apprehension, and as such is made visible to us. The question as to what reality is apart from these forms, and what are its independent attributes, becomes irrelevant here. For the mind, only that can be visible which has some definite form; but every form of existence has its source in some peculiar way of seeing, some intellectual formulation and intuition of meaning. Once language, myth, art and science are recognized as such forms, the basic philosophical question is . . . that of their mutual limitations and supplementation.[33]

Several volumes later Cassirer works out the meaning and interrelation of the several symbolic forms. Two of his three volumes on *The Philosophy of Symbolic Forms* are devoted to language and myth. His last work, *The Myth of the State,* is devoted to an analysis of political forms, with especial attention to the demonic myths of 20th-century man as exemplified by the totalitarian state. And, in *Essay on Man* he offers a brief overview of his total philosophic scheme. Trained in the humanities, and an expert in his early life on the epistemology of science, he has offered explicit and detailed treatment of each of the major cultural expressions of man—language, art, history, science, myth, and religion. He sees no reason to confine knowledge to science and to regard the other symbolic expressions of man as emotionalism, as the positivists would have us do. He provides a thoroughly convincing answer to modern positivism when he points out that science is merely one of several symbolic forms. He brings this out in his introduction to the three-volume *magnum opus* when he says "just as scientific theory is not to be judged by referring back to the experience which it reconstructs but by its own standards of theoretical completeness, so art is not to be judged in terms of its 'imitation' of perception. . . . There is no privileged status for science over art or any other symbolic formation which constitutes some kind of interpretation of experience." [34] Perhaps the key to Cassirer's epistemological argument lies in the stress which he places on mental activities[35] leading to meaning rather than attempting to develop an abstract criterion for the acceptance or rejection of some event as "truth."

His stress on the symbol as mental process allows him to look with more sympathy than would be the case for most epistemologists at the problem of knowledge as it relates to myth. The myth has been traditionally viewed as of little consequence from the point of view of theory of knowledge. In some quarters, notably among anthropologists and psychologists, it has been thought of as essentially pre-logical thought, a type of childish expression on the part of primitive minds. Perhaps the only scholars who have viewed the myth with favor are the specialists in literature and religion. But even among such scholars it has been difficult to elucidate the sense in which the myth is a conveyor of truth. It is at this point that Cassirer's insights are particularly significant, for he sees the myth as one of the many symbolic forms which have emerged from the culture of man. In fact, he sees the myth, along with language, as the parental source from which the other symbolic forms have evolved. In short, he sees myth as man's first expression to encompass the universe. But this expression is, by definition, relatively undifferentiated. If the myth is, in effect, the source from which such symbolic forms as science, art, and religion were developed, then we would expect the myth to be relatively amorphous and undeveloped. It is, therefore, a mixture of various symbolic forms, a totality which has in it certain scientific elements, certain artistic components, and religious components. And from the psychological view, from the viewpoint of the mental processes involved, it is a similarly non-pure mixture of thought, feeling, and intuition.

Both philosophically and psychologically, then, the myth represents man's attempt to encompass the whole of existence. But it does this in a relatively uncritical way, primarily because only by such openness can the myth represent the eternal verities concerning man and the universe in the face of flux and flow of historical circumstances, evolutionary events, and changes in our awareness of the nature of things. Relative amorphousness is, then, a must for this particular symbolic form, whether it emerges from the mind of so-called primitive man, or from the life and times of modern man. The amorphous, undifferentiated, and primal nature of myth is brought out by Cassirer in the preface to his volume on mythical thinking where he says:

> None of these forms [i.e., symbol systems] started out with an independent existence and clearly defined outlines of its own; in its beginnings, rather, every one of them was shrouded and disguised in some form of myth. There is scarcely any realm of "objective spirit" which cannot be shown to have entered at one time into this fusion, this concrete unity, with myth. The production of art and knowledge—the contents of ethics, law, language, and technology—all point to the same basic relationship. The question of the origin of language is indissolubly interwoven with that of the origin of myth; the one can be raised only in relation to the other. Similarly, the problem of the beginnings of art, writing, law, or science leads back to a stage in which they all resided in the immediate and undifferentiated unity of the mythical consciousness. Only very gradually do the basic theoretical concepts of knowledge (space, time, and number) or of law and social life (the concept of property, for example) or the various notions of economics, art and technology free themselves from this involvement.[36]

Thus, just as the infant slowly distinguishes himself from his environmental surroundings, eventually develops a consciousness of self, and finally emerges as an integrated but more differentiated unity, so early man has moved from an essentially intuitive-global approach to reality, through the breakdown of such intuitive approaches as the myth in its more differentiated components of science, art, and religion. The exact evolution of these symbolic forms, is, of course, not known, but Cassirer suggests that the underlying epistemological development is from direct sensation, to intuition, to conceptualization of an elementary nature, and finally, to true rational or logical judgment. This epistemological hierarchy implies greater and greater maturity in the sense that the subsequent development presupposes the preceding ones. Thus, logical judgment would be impossible without direct sensation at its base, but direct sensation does not necessarily require true logical judgment as a prerequisite. There is, then, an implication that those symbolic forms, such as art and science, which go beyond direct sensation and intuition represent more recently developed forms of symbolic expression. The fact that the mythical way of thinking is rather directly tied to the more "primitive" mental processes of sensation and intuition, or to "immediacy" as it relates to reality is seen from the following quote:

. . . this form of reality is still completely homogeneous and undifferentiated. Hence the nuances of significance and value which knowledge creates in its concept of the object, which enable it to distinguish different spheres of objects and to draw a line between the world of truth and the world of appearances, are utterly lacking. Myth lives entirely by the presence of its object—by the intensity with which it seizes and takes possession of consciousness in a specific moment. . . . Consciousness is bound by its mere facticity, it possesses neither the impulsion nor the means to correct or criticize what is given here and now, to limit its objectivity by measuring it against something not given, something past or future. And if this mediate criterion is absent, all "truth" and reality dissolve into the mere presence of the content, all phenomena are situated on a single plane. Here there are no different degrees of reality, no contrasting degrees of objective certainty. . . . Above all it lacks any fixed dividing line between mere "representation" and "real" perception, between wish and fulfillment, between image and thing. This is most clearly revealed by the crucial significance of dream experience in the genesis and growth of the mystical consciousness. . . . For mythical thinking and mythical "experience" there is always a hovering between the world of dream and the world of objective reality.[37]

The sense of complete identity with the object in terms of sensory and intuitive involvement, combined with the failure to differentiate between the dream world and the objective world, points up the primitive nature of mythical thought. It should be made clear that the word "primitive" is meant here in the sense of crude as opposed to sophisticated, global as opposed to specific, and, above all, concrete or sensory as opposed to abstract or rational, for there is no implication that early man's brain was any less capable of dealing with abstraction than that of contemporary man. In short, there is no evidence to support the notion that "modern man" has a biologically superior brain to that of "primitive man." In this connection Cassirer makes it clear that it is erroneous to associate the words "primitive man" and "myth" as if they were somehow synonymous. "For myth has not really been vanquished and subjugated. It is always there, lurking in the dark and waiting for its hour and opportunity. This hour comes as soon as the other binding forces of man's social life, for one reason or another, lose their strength and are no longer able to combat the demonic mythical powers." [38] His thesis is that the energy which is invested in the myth takes a political form in the modern day, whereas in antiquity such energy was usually directed toward religious concerns.

A convincing and hair-raising development of this theme is given by Eric Hoffer in his book *The True Believer*.[39] The "true believer" is a fanatic, the possessor of the one and only truth, who is ready to die for a cause. Hoffer makes the point that it does not particularly matter what the cause, just so it provides the opportunity for escape from a self the "true believer" no longer wants. Such "religiofication," the art of turning practical purposes or movement into holy causes, provides hope for the deeply frustrated. The "true believer" is a lost soul, a spiritual derelict of humanity, whose sense of meaninglessness is so overwhelming as to result in a complete shattering of the ego. Identification with a mass movement of some kind, whether it be labeled religious, social, or political, provides the vehicle for regaining a bigger and better self and thereby a sense of purpose and meaning. One way to fill one's spiritual emptiness is to ultimatize either in terms of an abstract idea such as Communism or Nazism, or in terms of individual heroes such as Hitler, Stalin, or Mussolini. Hitler, for example, was regarded by his most ardent followers as the Saviour of the German people, sent by God to lead them to the millennium. Psychologically, Hitler, as the New Messiah, served as a symbol of spiritual rebirth or psychological wholeness. However, since this type of identification represents a denial of self in the name of the group, thereby not allowing for the possibility of psychological growth, this type of religious involvement is idolatrous and demonic.

The point is that the myth deals optimally with the

group or collective concerns of man, and the modern
state has more of a hold on such concerns than does the
modern church. If, in fact, we bring in Jung's insight at
this point concerning modern man's spiritual emptiness,
and combine it with Tillich's concept of faith as ultimate
concern, it is easy to see the power of Cassirer's analysis
of the totalitarian state as a reflection of mythical thinking on the part of 20th-century man. Jung's demonstration of the importance of the hero archetype in mythical
thinking, for example, lends weighty support to the type
of analysis reflected in Cassirer's *Myth of the State*. In
fact, the thought of Jung, Cassirer, and Tillich converge
on this issue and point rather convincingly to the spiritual
needs of men of all time, as well as bring out the close
relationship between these needs and the emergence of
mythical thought.

Cassirer's analysis of the close relationship between the
myth and religion is relevant at this juncture. Part of this
analysis includes an evolutionary account of how religion,
while inextricably enmeshed with myth, actually goes beyond it as an independent form of symbolization. The
key to this development lies in the interplay between
artistic expression and the slow awareness of "self" as a
separate entity. Cassirer points out that in the mythical
thinking of antiquity there was a complete identification
of each member of the tribe with the tribal myth. That
is, there was no clear awareness of individual identity;
instead there was a feeling of fusion or oneness with the
tribal community and with the cosmos ("participation
mystique"), a feeling which was supported by the myth
of the time. He points out that the shift from a more
or less communal soul to a private self did not occur until
the development of an ethical consciousness:

> Out of the ethical-prophetic idea of the future grows a
> true discovery of man's individuality, of his personal self.
> Primitive mythical conceptions of the soul serve as a founda-
> tion for the discovery, but on this material an entirely new
> form is ultimately imprinted. Thus the mythical conscious-
> ness undergoes at this point a development which is destined
> to surpass its limits. In the history of Greek philosophy we
> can still follow in detail this gradual release of the specula-
> tive idea of the self from its native mythical soil. . . . It is

> achieved when the soul ceases to be a mere natural potency
> and apprehends itself as an ethical subject. Only now is man
> free from fear of the unknown, from the fear of demons,
> because he no longer feels that his self, his innermost being,
> is dominated by a dark mythical power but knows himself
> capable of molding this self from clear insight, through a
> principle of knowledge and will. Thus there arises in opposi-
> tion to myth a new consciousness of inner freedom. . . .
> Man now achieves his true self through self-responsibility.[40]

Cassirer feels that this evolution toward selfhood on
the part of man is reflected in the various art forms. He
points out, for example, that the Egyptians' changing
vision of man is evident in their plastic representation of
the gods as they shift from purely animal to human-
animal forms (e.g., a human body with the head of a
snake). The humanizing of the gods in Greek sculpture
and mythology was then carried several steps further.

Cassirer's clearest statement of the interplay between
artistic expression and increased self-consciousness lies in
his exposition of the evolution of certain literary forms.
This evolution moves from myth to epic, to tragedy, and
to drama in general. He points out, for example, that the
Greek tragedy is the first artistic form to see the "I" as
an independent and self-responsible agent. "In contrast
to the epic, tragedy shifts the center of events from outside in, and thus there arises a new form of ethical self-
consciousness, through which the gods take on a new
nature and form." [41] Thus, the self concept, the idea of
a separate and controllable personality, moves into consciousness. And what is more existentially powerful in the
annals of theatre than the Greek sense of guilt and
tragedy as one of their great works of dramatic literature
moves slowly and inexorably to its necessary conclusion!
It is doubtful that man shall ever evolve more powerful
portrayals of the ethical-tragic aspects of life than those of
the Greeks.

A major point which Cassirer makes in this development is that the dramatic literary form best conveys the
essence of the I-thou relationship which is necessary for
the development of selfhood. And, as Martin Buber[42] has
demonstrated, the I-thou relationship, as opposed to I-it,
lies at the base of religious consciousness. The I-thou

relationship, along with its underlying significance for self-awareness and religious awareness, is also evident in the anthropomorphic projection of multiple Greek gods. Cassirer sees this as further progress in the cultural evolution of man. "In the multiplicity of his gods man does not merely behold the outward divinity of natural objects and forces but also perceives himself in the concrete diversity and distinction of his functions. . . . Over and over again we thus find confirmation of the fact that man can apprehend his own being only insofar as he can make it visible in the image of his gods. . . ." [43]

The last portion of this quote from Cassirer—namely, "that man can apprehend his own being only insofar as he can make it visible in the image of his gods. . . ."—if properly understood, can be taken as a brief summary of what Jung has been trying to convey in his psychological studies of the myth. For Jung has been saying that the history of the development of the human psyche lies symbolically hidden in the major myths of mankind. The myth not only tells us about the outer reality of the cosmos, but it also reflects the inner reality of the psyche. For as the content of the myth progresses from many gods to one god, for example, man moves from relative unconsciousness to relative consciousness. In short, polytheism symbolically represents a multitude of fragmented ego projections which move toward a more unified "self" as the myth moves toward monotheism. This point can be grasped only if we see the myth as a product of the collective or group unconscious which is parallel to the dream as a product of the individual or personal unconscious. Just as the individual symbolically projects unconscious material to the surface via the dream, so collective or group concerns are unconsciously projected into consciousness via the myth. Thus, if we will make a psychological analysis of the metaphoric content of the myth in a manner comparable to the analyst's interpretation of a dream series, we will be led to a greater understanding of the nature of man's psyche. We will see, for example, that the archetypal hero represents everyman's search for wholeness (psychology), individuation (Jung), or salvation (religion). Thus, in the typical myth the hero must undergo fantastic pain, suffering, and essentially impossible

achievement before finally emerging victorious. The kill-
ing of the several dragons is comparable to the several
"deaths" and "rebirths" which are necessary if one is to
achieve a more differentiated and a more integrated
psyche. In more explicitly Jungian terms, such heroics are
symbolic of a more individuated psyche, one in which,
for example, one's dark side, moving into greater awareness, corresponds to the death and rebirth sequence.

In a similar view, Jung points out that alchemy can be
seen as meaningful; not as inadequate chemistry, but
rather, as a symbolic manifestation of the human thrust
for wholeness. The alchemist's desire to turn base metals
into gold is symbolic of his desire to transform his animal-
like nature into something more divine.[44] The same
theme is evident in all the major myths of man; from the
Babylonian epic of Gilgamesh, the great myths of the
east, and the Christian myth to the modern flying saucer
myth.[45] In all of them man unconsciously repeats the
same psychic need for self-awareness, which, in the more
refined religious myths, is projected with greatest depth
and meaning in the archetypal symbol of God.

How do we move beyond the myth to religion?

> Religion takes the decisive step that is essentially alien to
> myth: in its use of sensuous images and signs it recognizes
> them as such—a means of expression which, though they
> reveal a determinate meaning, must necessarily remain inade-
> quate to it, which "point" to this meaning but never wholly
> exhaust it. In the course of its development every religion
> comes to a point at which it must withstand this "crisis"
> and break loose from its mythical foundation. . . . For the
> religious significance of an event depends no longer on its
> content but solely on its form: what gives it its character
> as a symbol is not what it is and whence it immediately
> comes but the spiritual aspect in which it is seen, the rela-
> tion to the universe which it obtains in religious feeling and
> thought.[46]

In other words, as mythical thought moves from naïve
realism and literalism to symbolic awareness, it moves in
the direction of religious consciousness. As long as the
person is stuck with literalism, the sense that "this is it,"
not that this is symbolic of ultimate reality, but rather,
that this *is* ultimate reality, he is residing in the land of

myth. Clearly this is the predicament of fundamentalist religious sects, and, for that matter, of all institutionalized religions insofar as they insist upon literalism. In terms of the earlier sections of this chapter on sign and symbol, such religious commitments have erroneously taken a symbol for a sign. That is, they impose the one-for-one interpretation which is typical of the sign onto the one-for-many correspondence which is typical of the symbol. Thus, various events are taken as a "sign" of the presence of God, and various scriptures are seen as God's word in the literal sense. This mistaking of pre-ultimate symbols for *the* ultimate leads to idolatry, the ultimatizing of that which is, in fact, *not* ultimate.

Religious involvement demands that we break through the literalistic encapsulation of the myth and "see through it." Tillich speaks of a myth so viewed as a "broken myth," [47] meaning that it is no longer taken as the literal, absolute truth. The theologian Bultmann speaks of such religious growth as "demythologization," [48] that is, the "seeing through" or the "breaking" of the mythical aspects of religion. Clearly, such "demythologization" is currently taking place, at least in the religious traditions of the Western world. According to Bultmann, Tillich, and Cassirer such developments reflect a deeper religious awareness. However, such developments also reflect a severe crisis for the viability of the "demythologized" religion, as well as a sharp rise in the spiritual yearnings of mankind. It is at this point that the "true believer" is at his most dangerous. For he is most likely to re-commit himself, and whoever will follow, to a "reli-giofied," mass movement. In short, in such periods of value transition we must be on guard for the tendency of man's spiritual emptiness to manifest itself, not in true religious commitment, but rather, in pre-religious myth-making. The myth, then, must be seen in proper perspective as intertwined with religion, but not equivalent to it; it should be seen as a crude unconscious reaching for the deeper meanings of psychic and religious involvement, which may or may not be able to adequately contain such natural human yearnings.

The relation between the manifestations of myth and the spiritual emptiness of modern man is perhaps the major theme of C. G. Jung. His position is that modern man is in search of a soul [49] because the traditional religious symbols have lost their meaning. Jung interprets the increase of neuroticism in our time and the mass psychosis of modern totalitarianism as symptomatic of spiritual starvation. He interprets these mental disturbances as the natural compensatory activity of unconscious processes. He claims there is always an increase in "symbolizing" when the contemporary symbols fail to convey sufficient meaning. The result is an increase in symbolic representations in individual men's fantasies and dreams and an increase in mythmaking at the group level.

The most meaningful symbolic manifestations of man, whether observed at the individual level or in the analysis of myths, are the archetypes. These recurrent themes are so meaningful because they reflect the eternal needs of the psyche, they reflect the tendency toward wholeness, they reveal man's searching for the unity of his soul. The most powerful of these universal expressions of psychic need is the archetype of God. The symbol of God commands more psychic energy than any other archetypal symbol. In any hierarchical ordering of symbols this symbol falls at the top because it most adequately reflects the life-process. Symbols such as the sun and the bull also represent life forces, but not as powerfully as does the symbol of God. The central position of this archetype is brought out by Progoff when he says that ". . . the God-complex is the focus around which other symbols gather, and from it comes the energic force with which they may be vitalized into a 'lived' religion. . . . No constellation of symbols can function as a religion in the psyche unless its particular symbol for God is 'alive.' . . ." [50]

The point here is that a living religion is the dominant force which holds a social structure together. Since it is the core around which people build the meaning of their lives, by definition its symbols represent what a people value most. And if the God-symbol is no longer meaningful, it means a people has lost its faith. "To say that an individual has 'faith' is to say, psychologically, that he can live his symbols, that they are *alive* within him; and to say that an individual is 'sceptical' means that the symbols are no longer spontaneously active or alive within him." [51]

In other words, the contemporary man, living in a time of rapid social and political change and value confusion, is essentially faithless or sceptical. And so he consciously and unconsciously is casting about with considerable aimlessness in search of a value scheme and a meaningful set of symbols.

Jung's answer to the problem is for contemporary man to listen more attentively to the unconscious aspects of his psyche. He points out that Western man, for example, is too abstract and rational in his approach to life, and that his dark or unconscious side lies in the feeling or emotional aspects of life. Instead of repressing this aspect of our nature, Jung recommends that we allow unconscious yearnings to well up to the surface in a variety of symbolic forms as expressions of natural compensatory psychological processes. He points out that psychic opposites provide the tension which is the basis for psychic energy, and that psychic energy must eventually be released. And if it is not released in such a manner as to lead to psychic wholeness—that is, in terms of a more complete development of the four major psychological functions of thinking, feeling, sensation, and intuition— then the usual psychic aberrations will follow. The tendency of the psyche to move toward a state of integration or individuation must be viewed as a life-long task, but those who are "on the road" will presumably know it by the subsequent buoyancy of spirit which accompanies "wholeness." Thus, the implication is that if we will simply make the most of the unconscious we will be moving in the direction of greater psychological and religious awareness. The theologian Schaer accepts this position when he points out that "Religion is the acknowledgement of the things that consciousness fails to realize. . . . Religion contributes substantially to a man's total structure, and a living religion is needed for the full development of personality." [52] He accepts individuation as the key to rebirth and suggests that "the task of religion is to do what the symbol does: bring opposites together." [53]

It is important to note what has emerged in this exposition of the thought of Cassirer, Jung, and Tillich. As I see it, these three represent a complementary pattern branching out from a common point of departure. Their agreement stems from viewing symbolic and mythological products as resultants of mental activities, as ways in which the mind or the brain works on stimulus inputs. The difference in their views stems from the fact that Cassirer gives us an essentially conscious and evolutionary theory of symbolization, although he is obviously not opposed to unconscious processes; Jung gives us an essentially unconscious theory of symbolization, although he is not opposed to conscious processes; and Tillich, while open to both the conscious and unconscious components of symbolization, offers us a transcendent theory of the symbol. Finally, Cassirer offers us an all-encompassing philosophic framework as an explanation for the origin and development of symbolic outputs with asides to the underlying psychological process—hence, the reference to Cassirer's system as an anthropological philosophy. Jung, on the other hand, offers us an all-pervading psychology of symbolic processes infiltrated with rich philosophical implications. Tillich, completely aware of the philosophical and psychological aspects of the symbol and the myth, is primarily concerned that they be viewed within the context of the transcendent or the religious, and with application to the existential aspect of the human predicament. We emerge with a penetrating analysis of possibly the deepest and most important aspect of man.

THE PHILOSOPHY OF "AS IF"

How can we best sum up what we have been trying to say about the symbol and the myth as they relate to reality? It has been estimated that our universe, one of an unknown, but very large number of universes, is around 6 billion years of age. It has been estimated that our sun, one of thousands of millions of stars, is around 5 billion years of age. And it has been estimated that our earth, one of countless planets, is around 4 billion years old.[54] It has been estimated that life has existed on earth for the past 2 to 3 billion years and that man has been on the scene for 1,500,000 of these years. Recorded history is only five to six thousand years old. The first "high" civilizations of which we are aware occurred in

Egypt, Mesopotamia, and the Indus Rivers around 4,000 B.C. From this time until around 300 to 200 B.C. our conception of the universe was stated in the essentially unconscious-intuitive form of the myth. At this time, primarily under the leadership of Eastern thinkers and mystics such as Confucius and Lao Tse in China, Buddha in India, Zarathustra in Persia, and old testament prophets in Palestine, and such Greek thinkers as Homer, Plato, and Thucydides, man became more and more aware of himself and of his place in the cosmos. In short, he began to evidence spiritual concerns. From around 800 to 200 B.C. until the time of the Renaissance (A.D. 1500), concern for the spirit dominated the mind of man. From the time of the Renaissance (A.D. 1500) until the present (20th century A.D.), man's world-view changed from an essentially spiritual outlook to an essentially scientific outlook. The cosmologies or conceptions of the universe which men held during these three major periods of recorded history can be briefly referred to as the mythological (early man to 6th century B.C.), the geocentric-finite or Ptolemaic (6th century B.C. to Renaissance), and the heliocentric or Copernican (Renaissance to 20th century A.D.). The most popular contemporary cosmology is some form of expanding universe (e.g., Hubble-Einstein).[56]

How, in the face of just these few superficial items covering the history of man and of his relative insignificance in terms of space and time, how can man have the egotistical gall to announce to the universe that he knows ultimate reality? Granted that he psychologically requires a world-view, why does he so readily allow this view to slide over the epistemological barrier (see Chapter 2) and emerge later as ultimate truth? Surely the world-viewer who will at least review the facts just cited will retreat with a little humility. Surely we have learned that whatever our conception of reality, that conception is not to be confused with the thing itself. The major point of this chapter is that the symbol, the myth, or any other cultural form, is essentially an analogy or a metaphor which mediates between man, the subjective knower, and reality, the objective unknowable. It would be difficult to deny the validity of Vaihinger's philosophy of "As If"[56] at this juncture. He demonstrates that man requires useful fictions in all approaches to knowledge, including science, because these useful fictions help us so effectively in trying to understand the nature of things it is "as if" they were "true." Similarly, the literary critic Kenneth Burke sees symbols as "strategies for encompassing situations."

I see the reality of the myth and the symbol, then, in the same way that I would eventually test the reality of any symbolic form—according to the principle of existential validity. If it helps man to navigate through life, particularly if it does this in a way which maximizes meaningfulness, then it should be regarded as "real." If the item in question lends itself to some abstract principle for checking on its validity, such as is the case for the problem of scientific truth, it is simply easier to apply the abstract principle rather than turn to the more difficult job of checking it out existentially. But if the item in question is less literalistic than science or mathematics (that is, more symbolic, such as a great play, a novel, or a work of art or music), then we are forced to apply the more difficult and vaguer criterion of meaningfulness to life.

When men pool their existentially valid findings and project them out into the universe and ask the ultimate questions of life, when they, in effect, try to encompass the totality of things, they are, in my opinion, offering a mythological statement concerning the nature of reality. And it is my view that the best they can muster is an image of this totality—a reality image, or a myth. It happens that the view which is currently accepted as "really" real is the image we gain from the scientific community. That is, science is what is really believed in these days. Science, therefore, is in danger of becoming ultimatized or mythologized. Science is in danger of religiofication, the art of turning a secular matter into a religion. As long as science remains in the hands of the scientists and confines itself to the relatively limited perspective of reality of which it is capable, there is no danger. However, when science is picked up by the "true believer" and turned into "scientism," that is, when it is extended beyond its natural boundaries in an effort to answer the questions of ultimate reality, then we have the makings of a new myth. There are strong indications that this has already occurred to a considerable extent. It is powerfully revealed in the essential distrust with which academicians view non-scientific disciplines, and it is equally powerfully revealed in the extent to which non-scientific disciplines ape the sciences. It is also equally manifest in the general population by the fact that both Russia and the United States find that they can speak most convincingly to the world via a display of scientific and technological know-how. Whatever myth is current is, of course, the most dangerous. For the current myth is mankind's best available statement at the moment as to "the way things really are." And the truth is not really open to serious question because it is so obviously the truth.

Scientism is a real danger in today's world. The avoidance of this kind of religious commitment represents the most serious challenge to those of the "creative minority" who would escape the evils of encapsulation and idolatry. Unless we are alert, history may record that our peers of the 30th century, in looking back at the "primitive" peoples of the 20th century, were impressed by our relatively advanced "scientific myth" concerning the nature of ultimate reality.

NOTES

1. Suzanne Langer, *op. cit.*, p. 20.

2. E. A. Hoebel (editor), *Readings in Anthropology*, New York: McGraw-Hill, 1955.

3. Ernst Cassirer, *An Essay on Man*, New York: Doubleday & Co., 1956, pp. 43-45.

4. For example, see H. F. Harlow, The development of learning in the Rhesus monkey, *American Scientist*, 1959, *47*, 459-479.

5. See especially the publications of such psychologists as Robert Yerkes, K. S. Lashley, and Henry Nissen.

6. See the recent semi-popular book by Cathy and Keith Hayes, *The Ape in Our House*, New York: Harper, 1951, and the earlier, more technical study by W. N. Kellogg, *The Ape and the Child*, New York: McGraw-Hill Book Company, Inc., 1933.

7. In a variety of experimental reports emanating primarily from the Roscoe B. Jackson Memorial Laboratory, Bar Harbor, Maine, including my own research along these lines. See, for example, J. R. Royce and W. K. Silvers, A preliminary report

on the barrel, rope, and post test. *J. of Genetic Psychology*, 1954, *84*, 299-309.

8. Summarized in N. R. F. Maier and T. C. Schnierla, *Principles of Animal Psychology*, New York: McGraw-Hill, 1935.

9. The reference to Helen Keller brought forth the following perceptive comment on freedom and encapsulation from one of my critical readers, Robert Kimball. "What an example of a type of encapsulation, and yet a freeing of the self from bonds that are nevertheless not removed." Kimball's statement constitutes a succinct expression of existential freedom within the context of determined limitations. (See the discussion of free will on pp. 118-122.)

10. Helen Keller, *The Story of My Life*, New York: Doubleday & Company, Inc., 1902, 1903. Supplementary account of Helen Keller's life and education, pp. 315.

11. J. B. Wolfe, Effectiveness of Token-Rewards for Chimpanzees, *Comparative Psychol. Monog.*, *12*, No. 5.

12. Helen Keller, *op. cit.*

13. Several writers have made a parallel distinction between sign and symbol in terms of denotative and connotative meaning. If we cast our thinking in terms of the standard S-O-R paradigm of contemporary theoretical psychology, our conceptual focus would lie at the S-O end of the continuum. We should then classify all incoming stimuli in terms of signs or symbols depending upon the subsequent meaning-mediational process. Signs (e.g., the conditioned response) would be characterized by such words as denotative, specific cues, cognitive, and cortical; in short, such stimuli-meanings reflect one-to-one correspondences. Symbols (e.g., a country's flag) would be characterized by such words as connotative, diffuse cues, affective, and cortical-subcortical; in short, such stimuli-meanings reflect one-to-many correspondences. It is fortunate that the psychologist C. E. Osgood (see *The Measurement of Meaning*, authored with G. J. Suci and P. H. Tannenbaum, Urbana: University of Illinois Press, 1957) has devised a method for empirically attacking the multiple meanings of symbolic material. His method, known as the semantic differential, involves the application of factor analysis to ratings of stimuli on a seven-point scale. He finds that he can account for most of the semantic variance in terms of the permutations and combinations of a three-dimensional system. The dimensions are labeled evaluative (good-bad, fair-unfair), potency (strong-weak, masculine-feminine), and active (excitable-calm, quick-slow). Osgood's contribution is of considerable importance, for it now gives the psychologist empirical leverage on the problem of semantic meaning, a problem which has been essentially re-

fractory to empirical investigation. It is also of considerable theoretical importance, for his thinking is offered within the tradition of an objective, experimental psychology, without doing violence to the nuances of the word meaning. In short, his representational-mediation model of meaning is both theoretically sound and experimentally feasible—no mean achievement for so difficult a problem.

14. Leslie White, *op. cit.*, p. 304.

15. For a full treatment of the archetypal hero, see Joseph Campbell, *The Hero of a Thousand Faces*, New York: Pantheon Book, 1949.

16. His "team" or helpers.

17. The *barrera* is the wall which circles the arena and contains the bull.

18. It is said of Manolete, who openly confessed to fear when asked if he experienced it in the bullring, that he never *showed* it during a fight.

19. Corrida literally means "running." A bullfight in Spanish is a Corrida de Toros—literally, a running of bulls.

20. The term toreador is incorrect. It is used by aficionados to identify an inferior torero or bullfighter.

22. C. S. Hall, *The Meaning of Dreams*, New York: Harper & Bros., 1953, p. 10.

23. Ruth Monroe, *Schools of Psychoanalytic Thought*, New York: Dryden Press, 1955, p. 64.

24. The problems surrounding analysis of the symbol are vast. This subject has been examined by scholars representing all the major segments of knowledge, especially the disciplines of psychology, anthropology, philosophy, theology, literature, and science. Thus, it should be obvious that my treatment of this problem in the present context cannot reflect an adequate coverage of the many issues involved. For example, this presentation is not at all adequate from the mythological-anthropological point of view, nor have the views of literary critics or scientists been adequately represented. Let it suffice to say that I have presented my point of view on the symbol, particularly as it relates to the major theme of this book. I know of no statement on this subject which is adequate to the complexities of the task. In this section, in particular, I sample only one psychologist, one philosopher, and one theologian. But the contributions of these three important thinkers on this subject converge in this context. It is my hope that the point of view which emerges will represent at least one valid aspect of the total problem. For a further sampling of relevant statements see J. R. Royce (editor), *Multidisciplinary Analysis of the Symbol: Implications for Psychology*, New York: Random House (in press).

25. Jung's concept of self-realization. Individuation is discussed at greater length in Chapter 9.

26. J. G. Miller, *Unconsciousness*, New York: John Wiley, 1942.

27. Because of the confusion which surrounds Jung's thinking on the concept of archetype, particularly as it relates to whether archetypes reflect learned material or whether they are somehow innate (see also p. 173), the writer will make an explicit disclaimer at this juncture. The writer is *not* affirming that ideas are somehow inherited. What the writer would defend is that a bodily constitution, including a brain, *is* inherited, and that it is natural for a brain to symbolize, both at the conscious and the unconscious levels. The fact that the brains of men have symbolically produced (i.e., via dreams and myths) similar images in different cultures is an interesting phenomenon. Jung has conceptualized this observation under the rubric of archetypes, and he has postulated the collective unconscious as the source of such symbolic manifestations. (See pages 153-155, 173-174.) The relevance of hereditary mechanisms as opposed to cultural conditioning as determinants of archetypal phenomena is simply unknown, and the idea of the inheritance of acquired characteristics was convincingly annihilated at least fifty years ago. It is unfortunately true that Jung's writings are primarily responsible for the confusion on this issue. For he has written different things at different times and places, sometimes actually claiming that archetypes are inherited, and at other times disclaiming such an idea. Regardless of Jung's personal confusion on this matter, there is no convincing scientific evidence available to help us decide on the adequacy of the concept of collective unconsciousness. The facts regarding various symbolic products are there, but a convincing explanation to account for such phenomena does not exist. Jung's concept of collective unconscious should, therefore, be regarded as a useful theoretical construct, an abstraction which is descriptive of certain behavioral observations.

28. See, for example, C. G. Jung and C. Kerenyi, *Essays on a Science of Mythology*, Bollingen Series XXII, New York: Pantheon Books, 1952. In general, Jung's writings are discursive and unsystematic. Therefore, for an introductory summary I recommend a systematic compilation such as will be found in Jolanda Jacobi, *The Psychology of C. G. Jung*, Revised Edition, New Haven: Yale University Press, 1943, or Frieda Fordham, *An Introduction to Jung's Psychology*, London: Penguin Books, 1953. Perhaps the most readable introductory writings by Jung himself can be found in *Modern Man in Search of a Soul*, New York: Harcourt, Brace & Co., 1953;

The Undiscovered Self, New York: Mentor Books, 1959; and the recent Modern Library compilation, *The Basic Writings of C. G. Jung*, New York: Random House, 1959.

29. Paul Tillich, *Dynamics of Faith*, pp. 41-43.

30. *Ibid.*, p. 53.

31. Paul Tillich, Existential analysis and religious symbols. In Will Herberg, *Four Existentialist Theologians*, New York: Doubleday & Co., 1958, p. 291.

32. Paul Tillich, *Dynamics of Faith*, p. 43.

33. Ernst Cassirer, *Language and Myth*, New York: Harper & Row, 1946, pp. 8-9.

34. Ernst Cassirer, *The Philosophy of Symbolic Forms*, New Haven: Yale University Press, 1955, Vol. II, *Mythical Thinking*, pp. xiv-xv.

35. Note the similarity in the psychological approach to epistemological problems between Cassirer and the writer as exemplified by Figure 2 and the elaboration of this figure in Chapter 2.

36. Ernst Cassirer, *Philosophy of Symbolic Forms*, pp. xiv-xv.

37. *Ibid.*, pp. 35-36.

38. Ernst Cassirer, *The Myth of the State*, New York: Doubleday & Co., 1955, p. 352.

39. Eric Hoffer, *The True Believer*, New York: Mentor Books, 1951.

40. Ernst Cassirer, *Philosophy of Symbolic Forms*, II, pp. 171-173.

41. *Ibid.*, p. 198.

42. Martin Buber, *I and Thou*, Second Edition, New York: Charles Scribner's Sons, 1958.

43. Ernst Cassirer, *Philosophy of Symbolic Forms*, II, pp. 204 and 218.

44. C. G. Jung, *Psychology and Alchemy*: Vol. XII of *Collected Works*, edited by Herbert Lead and others, New York: Pantheon Books, 1953.

45. C. J. Jung, *Flying Saucers, A Modern Myth of Things Seen in the Skies*, New York: Harcourt, Brace & Co., 1959.

46. Ernst Cassirer, *Philosophy of Symbolic Forms*, II, pp. 239 and 260.

47. Paul Tillich, *Systematic Theology*, *op. cit.*

48. R. Bultmann, New testament and mythology. In H. W. Bartsch, *Kerygma and Myth*, London: Billings and Sons, 1957, pp. 1-16.

49. Jung, C. G., *Modern Man in Search of a Soul*, New York: Harcourt, Brace, and Co.

50. Progoff, I., *Jung's Psychology and its Social Meaning*, New York: Grove Press, 1955, p. 214.

51. *Ibid.*, pp. 209-210.

52. H. Schaer, *Religion and the Cure of Souls in Jung's Psychology*, New York: Pantheon Books, 1950, p. 136.

53. *Ibid.*, p. 110.

54. See C. A. Coulson, *The Age of the Universe*, in Anchor Review #1, A64, New York: Doubleday and Company, 1955, pp. 235-252.

55. M. K. Munitz, *Theories of the Universe*, Glencoe: The Free Press, 1957.

56. H. Vaihinger, *The Philosophy of 'As If,'* London: Routledge and Kegan Paul, 1924.

9

The Unencapsulated Man

"Indeed, I do not forget that my voice is but one voice, my experience a mere drop in the sea, my knowledge no greater than the visual field in a microscope, my mind's eye a mirror that reflects a small corner of the world, and my ideas—a subjective confession."

—C. G. JUNG

"Awareness is the moment of crisis between seeing the transcience of the world with sorrow and regret, and seeing it as the very form of the Great Void."

—ALAN WATTS

The essence of encapsulation is to offer *one* approach to reality as if it were *the* approach. This results in the pronouncement that the ultimate nature of man and the universe is clearly understood and that we will all be saved if we will but listen and learn the word. We have seen that this kind of behavior is highly typical of men in all walks of life and in all times and places. Perhaps the essence of the tragedy of man is the conflict between his animal-like nature which holds him to the ground and his divine-like nature which demands that he transcend himself. If man must attempt to comprehend ultimate reality —and it appears that in some way, no matter how elemental or pagan, he must—then it will be necessary for him to break through the several cocoons within which he is inevitably encapsulated and broaden his "reality image."

The first step in this process is to recognize that he is encapsulated. It has been the aim of this book to aid this process by pointing out that contemporary man is not sufficiently aware—that he is limited, closed, finite, unthinking, unfeeling, insensitive—in short, that he is too unconscious! Unfortunately, de-encapsulation demands that we be able to get inside and outside of ourselves, our culture, and our time. This, we know, is impossible to attain completely. But it follows that if we become sufficiently aware of the problem, we will at least have a direction, a line of attack.

BOUNDLESS MIND

There is, of course, an underlying assumption that the unencapsulated man is preferable to the encapsulated man. It may be, after all, that the depth and extensiveness of creativity which would be released in an unencapsulated civilization would be so overwhelming as to drive us back into our pleasant little cocoons of ignorance and non-creativity. It may be that greater and greater visions of reality would be too much for the souls of men, and that such "seeing through" would drive them mad.[1] My position on this point is that despite this risk, the relatively untapped mind of 20th-century man contains endless possibilities, and that we must at least remain open to new ways of experiencing. Just as a backward glance points to great cultures which have emerged from the time of the ancient civilizations of Egypt and Mesopotamia, so a forward look suggests that the process of psycho-cultural differentiation has not been concluded. Just as outer space looks boundless to essentially earthbound men, so a glance inwardly suggests a similar feeling of ignorance and untapped resources concerning the nature of "mind." I personally get the same eerie experience of infinity when I contemplate the edges of mind as when I contemplate what appears to be the infinity of time and space. Whereas the Greeks thought of the basic unit of astronomical space as planetary, and 19th-century astronomy shifted to stars, we are currently thinking in terms of galaxies. But our galaxy is presumably just one out of a hundred million others of approximately the same size. If we add to this already inconceivable information the idea that the universe is continuously expanding, and if we do not come up with an impression of infinity concerning outer space, we must at least conclude that the firmament is sufficiently large as to be beyond our present comprehension.

What happens when we focus on the ten billion neurons of the brain? It would appear that we ought to be better off since we can at least get at this neural tissue. But it has always been true that man has understood his outer environment better than his inner environment. This predicament is poignantly illustrated in a recent cartoon which is reproduced as Figure 13. In fact the

Progress?

Fig. 13. Progress in inner space and outer space (By permission of Newspaper Enterprise Association)

history of the sciences clearly proceeded from the outside in—that is, from the outer world to the inner world. Historically, the physical sciences—astronomy, physics, geology, and chemistry—were developed first, followed by advances in the biological sciences, and only in the 19th and 20th centuries does man finally get around to the psychological and social sciences. The universe is by no means within his grasp, but man himself is generally conceded to be the riddle of all riddles. Unfortunately, although much has been learned concerning man's brain and his behavior, we cannot adequately explain the neural basis of a simple thought, we do not understand the relationship between the metabolism of the brain and behavior, and we cannot provide the physiological basis for intelligence. In short, we do not know how the brain is organized, nor how this organization relates to normal, supernormal, subnormal, and abnormal behavior. This kind of ignorance concerning man could be multiplied at great length, particularly if we move into highly important areas such as motivation and emotion. If we then contemplate the newly opened door of unconscious processes and creativity as untapped resources for aiding the de-encapsulation process, we are appalled by what we could accomplish if we merely proceeded in terms of what we already know, no less in terms of what we still have to learn. My point is that the inner space of mind, that is, the possibilities for the future emergence of new and modified symbolic forms, appear as limitless as the extension of outer space. Consider, for instance, the relevance of the recent developments in mathematics and logic. A perfect example of encapsulation in this field revolves around the fifth postulate of Euclid concerning the assumption that parallel lines do not meet. Operating within this and other pre-suppositions, the field of mathematics has been essentially Euclidean for over 2,000 years. The break from this development did not occur until the 19th century with an assumption, directly opposite to Euclid's fifth postulate, to the effect that parallel lines may meet. This shift in thought has resulted in a veritable revolution in mathematics, having unleashed a rash of "higher algebras," such as matrix theory, theory of groups, and other varieties of set theory. Classical mathematics has been rather closely tied to physical conceptions of time and space; the newer developments depart into conceptions involving time-space equivalents and a type of n-dimensional geometry which simply cannot be spatially visualized. Similar developments have occurred in recent decades in the development of what is called multi-valued logic as opposed to the traditional two-valued or Aristotelian true-false logic on which our present procedures rest.

The point to be made in both of these cases is that the successful prosecution of an intellectual line of endeavour can very easily fixate us on that particular approach. It is easy to become rigidified or set in the way things are to be accomplished. In short, it is easy to forget that any approach in any domain of knowledge is based on certain assumptions which are usually lost in antiquity, and rarely, if ever, reviewed and critically examined. The mathematicians and logicians of the last century have brilliantly demonstrated that when this is done, when different assumptions are tried on as a basis for subsequent logical deduction, a fascinating and very great variety of mathematical and logical systems emerge. Thus, a very broad horizon has reopened in an area which most people have long regarded as essentially closed and stabilized.[2]

A similar freezing of viewpoint can be demonstrated for all the current disciplines of knowledge. The *Zeitgeist* will simply not allow us to entertain ideas which are too alien to the spirit of the times; it is too confusing and upsetting in terms of the going world-view. This kind of encapsulation is what lies behind Renaissance man's intolerance of the heretical views of a Galileo who would remove man's earth from the center of the universe, and it is what lies behind the inability of a rational Victorian era to accept the irrationality which is implied in the insights of a Freud. Studies in the field of social psychology and anthropology are making us more aware of how we are victims of this particular acculturation process. More relevant at this point are the findings of the *gestalt* psychologists, who have clearly shown that the way we perceive determines how we state the problem and how we go about solving it. Wertheimer, for example, in his book on *Productive Thinking*,[3] points out how we fail to solve problems because of essentially rigidified approaches. He makes the important point that we can frequently do better if we will make our initial perception of the problem in terms of the total configuration rather than the more usual part approach. The point is also made that flexibility, both in terms of method of attack and in terms of providing a variety of hypotheses, is extremely important. The wide variety of intellectual and personality factors which are involved in creative thinking is just beginning to be probed by psychologists. But the story which has emerged so far suggests that the number of components will be over one hundred, and that the interactions and permutations and combinations involved in creative approaches in the various arts and sciences is fantastically complex. When the psychologist Thurstone first discovered the Primary Mental Abilities as recently as 1938 he was able to identify only seven components of intelligence with assurance. Since that date hundreds of such factors have been identified. For example, there are over 30 aptitude factors known for the comparatively simple task of flying an airplane. The many varieties of intellectual and creative abilities are just beginning to be discovered.[4]

Similar examples of untapped, partially because unknown, mental resources can be given concerning sensory processes. We once thought there were five senses; it is now known that there are some 21 different receptors specialized for the pick-up of one or another kind of physical energy. But we still do not know exactly how many different kinds of receptors mediate the perception of color, in spite of a monumental lifetime tome on the retina.[5] Neither is it certain what kind of sensory apparatus guides pigeons home, nor how birds navigate in general. The bird's brain is notoriously limited, so that it can hardly be attributed to some mysterious higher mental function, although a fantastic and fascinating variety of theories regarding bird navigation is present in the literature.[6] The answer to this mystery is most likely to be sensory, perhaps analogous to the radar-like ability which was discovered as the basis for night flying in bats and the sonar-like echo-location underwater directional ability of fish. In both of these examples the animal emits sounds which bounce back. The animal finds his way around on the basis of sound discrimination rather than visually or in terms of some higher intelligence. The point to be made here is that men do not use their senses any more than they use their heads. They do not use what they already have, and there is probably more they do not even know how to use. The stock example of man's failure to use his senses is that of the highly developed auditory acuity of blind persons as compared with the non-blind. The reason their auditory skills are so acute is that the necessity for developing them has been forced upon them. They have been attentive to sound stimuli for a long time, whereas the non-blind can adapt to similar situations by the more direct visual sensitivity. We are making a plea for men to move in the direction of developing the visual acuity of the deaf and the auditory sensitivity of the blind. In other words, we are making a plea for greater awareness.

LEVELS OF AWARENESS

The suggestion that men need to become more aware poses the question of their capacity to "take in" reality. The implication is that they live their lives in terms of highly restricted reality images, that there is much of which they are not conscious. Average men, those of the uncreative majority, live out their lives in an essentially unconscious or animal-like manner, working like robots from 9 to 5, mechanically eating and transporting, being dulled by television nightly, and mouthing the sounds which are piped into their brains by subtle motivation researchers, yellow journalists, and other special interest propagandists. A few men, the "creative minority," see through the various facets of life, the obvious ones of acculturation, and the deeper ones of self and destiny, and frequently provide us with new visions of reality. Such men, the creators of the arts and sciences, the inventors and the innovators, are the ones who are alive, perceptive, conscious. What is the nature of such super-consciousness? How much more conscious than mass man is a Hemingway, a Picasso, or an Einstein? And do the great seers and mystics of East and West see even more than an Einstein? If so, how?

In spite of the knowledge which has been gained in the last fifty years concerning such phenomena as hypnosis, sleep, anesthesia, and dreams, we are still profoundly ignorant concerning unconscious processes. Although the 19th century defined psychology as the study

of the normal, adult, *conscious* mind, we are similarly
ignorant about so-called conscious processes. Despite this
ignorance, however, psychologists, psychoanalysts, philosophers, and religionists have accumulated faint understand-
ings which can be related to one another. I propose to
bring out the relationships between different levels of
consciousness, which can be thought of as varying on a
continuum from complete non-awareness to complete
awareness, by reference to Figure 14.

Omniscience _____	Ultimate Consciousness (?)
Unencapsulated Man _____	Individuated Consciousness
Encapsulated Man _____	Specialized Consciousness
Mass Man _____	Collective Consciousness
Sentient Structures _____	Threshold of Consciousness
Symbolic Forms _____	Personal Unconsciousness
Primordial Images _____	Collective Unconsciousness
Free Energy _____	Ultimate Unconsciousness (?)

Fig. 14. The awareness continuum

Let us begin at the bottom of the figure with the concept of ultimate unconsciousness. It will be noted that
there is a similar concept, ultimate consciousness, at the
top of the chart. Both terms are followed by a question
mark in order to make it clear that such ultimate questions cannot be given ultimate answers.

Thus, while the nature of ultimate unconsciousness
cannot be ascertained, it can be hypothesized and brought
into relationship with other levels of consciousness. The
answer to the question of ultimate unconsciousness is unknowable because when pushed far enough, it becomes
the question of the origin of the universe. Obviously nobody has the answer concerning origin and destination,
but several reasonable cosmological theories have been
proposed. Most of them are in agreement that the ultimate nature of things can be described as undifferentiated
matter or energy—that is, an energy source out of which
elemental and more complex forms can be organized. I
am suggesting that some such amorphous energy pool can
probably be equated with what I have labeled ultimate
unconsciousness at the bottom of Figure 14. Out of this
undifferentiated source of energy, via inorganic and or-

ganic evolution, a great variety of forms became manifest
over a period of millions of years. Thus, more complex
forms, from the atom and the molecule to the crystal, the
virus, the amoeba and man, emerged (i.e., Bergson's
emergent evolution). The most complex of these forms
we speak of as life. "Non-live" manifestations of originally
undifferentiated energy carry the seeds of consciousness,
but so far as we know, are not themselves conscious.
While the exact point of emergence of consciousness is
not known, it would appear that life in some form is a
prerequisite.

If we equate consciousness with discriminability,[7] then
we should have to attribute a low degree of consciousness
or awareness to even the simplest single-celled animal
such as the amoeba or the paramecium. If we insist that
our discriminations must be verbalized, then, by definition, we restrict consciousness to man. The former hypothesis makes more sense to me and implies that consciousness begins with the simplest form of life and
increases as we ascend the phylogenetic series. Such an
increase in awareness implies a greater and greater flexibility in adapting to the environment. Perhaps the most
fundamental mode of adapting to the environment is by
means of instincts. Without such unlearned behavior patterns life could not continue because of failure of the
species to reproduce itself.

While of great importance to lower animal forms, instincts make up very little of man's total behavior repertoire. However, Jung has suggested a type of behavior
which, if it is not actually instinctive, is very close to it.
I am referring to his concept of the collective unconscious, the products of which, primordial images or archetypes, are considered to be universal (i.e., transcultural),
unlearned (i.e., "instinctual") phenomena. Jung's point
is that archetypal material manifests itself in a manner
exactly comparable to instinctive behavior patterns. Just
as the spider cannot help but spin webs, and is, so far as
we know, not conscious of such activity, so man unconsciously symbolizes his deepest inner concerns in his
dreams and myths. Man's bodily structure is the vessel
through which archetypes are expressed, just as the
spider's bodily structure is the vessel through which webs

are woven. The point is that the collective or objective unconscious transcends the personal unconscious. It may contain symbolic material of relevance to a particular psyche, but more importantly, it contains representations which have meaning for all men. These meanings are not meanings of the conscious mind; rather, they are meanings of the unconscious mind, best manifested in myths. Of course, man is not conscious of the current myth as myth; he unconsciously accepts it as "the way things are."

Whether or not Jung's conception will hold up, there simply is no rival statement on the matter, and it does provide us with a rather important link between the personal unconscious and the unknown ultimate unconscious. (See Figure 14.) Thus, we move from complete amorphousness, in the form of a pool of energy, to dim awareness, under the rubric of collective unconsciousness, to a very significant step toward the emergence of consciousness, the personal unconscious. I say a very significant step because true consciousness makes its first appearance at this level. H. B. English[8] defines the personal unconscious as "Two classes of activities: formerly conscious processes (or the representative of those processes) that have been expelled from the realm of the conscious; and certain primordial and infantile wishes and impulses that have never gained access to the conscious realm." The point is that the first class of activities refers to psychic contents which were once part of conscious awareness. Such contents were presumably forced into the unconscious[9] because they represented too much reality for the ego to assimilate comfortably. It is at this juncture that Freud offers his most ingenious insights, for he spells out how the defense mechanisms (repression, regression, projection, reaction formation, etc.) *unconsciously* deny, falsify, and distort reality. He points out, for example, that a temper tantrum on the part of an adult, or the necessity for a man to remain in bed while his mother-in-law visits, can serve to protect a badly exposed ego. Such regressive behavior (i.e., behavior which is more appropriate to an earlier age level) can sometimes be quite extreme, such as curling up in a ball, not speaking, or, in other words, symbolically returning to the mother's womb. Such behavior is protective, or ego preserving, and the underlying mechanisms of adjustment function at an unconscious level. It would appear that the organism "knows" what to do under stress, but the question is whether the ego "knows" what the organism is doing. Usually not. And, in fact, this is exactly where the psychoanalyst comes in, as a guide and counsellor, an aid in helping the client cut through the various defenses which perpetuate blindness, in the hope of bringing forth insight or greater self-awareness.

The most conscious of the various unconscious states is that degree of unawareness which is described as subliminal, or sub-threshold. At this level the person may make correct discriminations without being aware of the basis on which the discriminations are made. He may, for example, choose a certain color or sound correctly, even though the color is not visible or the sound audible. Or, he may choose the correct turn in a road on the basis of subliminal cues. The most convincing demonstration of subliminal behavior is that of a psychologist who experimentally produced unconscious conditioning.[10] In this experiment the subject was trained to give a conditioned response to the sound of a buzzer while under the influence of an anesthetic. Upon emerging from the unconscious state the person was presented with the bell stimulus. The subject gave the same conditioned response which had been elicited while under anesthesia. Similar demonstrations have been made during hypnosis and in post-hypnotic suggestions. Recent experiments on learning while asleep suggest a similar low level of consciousness.

Subliminal awareness is literally at the threshold of consciousness, that hazy range of no-man's land where one is half asleep, in a trance, or in a high state of emotion. As we pass over this threshold, it seems natural and proper to ask what consciousness is and how it differs from subliminal consciousness and the dimmer awareness of the personal and collective unconscious. The question of what consciousness is obviously cannot be answered with precision. English,[11] for example, devotes two entire pages of his dictionary to various definitions and, in effect, concludes that the term is essentially impossible to define. E. G. Boring, in the most scientific treatment of the sub-

ject that I know of, comes to conclusions which I see as
not inconsistent with our development. He sees consciousness as cognitive, having to do with knowledge and meanings. The key to it is the making of discriminations. In
short, if one can make discriminations, he is conscious;
if he cannot, he is unconscious.[12]

My position is that as we cross the threshold of consciousness we remain on the consciousness-unconscious-
ness continuum rather than move into a qualitatively
different realm. In terms of the evolutionary process, the
biological bases for making discriminations are more differentiated, that is, structurally more complex. More
specifically, as we ascend the animal kingdom phylogenetically, man simply has better structural equipment
for making discriminations—for example, better rods and
cones, a better auditory apparatus, and most importantly,
a more differentiated brain. This position implies a degree
of consciousness for animal life lower than man's, the
level of such consciousness to be roughly equated with
extent of biological differentiation. The dog, for example,
can hear sounds at higher frequencies than can man.
Whenever the underlying biological structure is superior,
we can anticipate superior discriminatory performances,
and to that extent, attribute consciousness to the dis-
criminator. Thus, it would appear reasonable to conclude
that conscious processes evolved out of unconscious
processes, both phylogenetically and developmentally;
phylogenetically, primarily in terms of the evolution of
brain structure, and developmentally, both in terms of
greater awareness as we grow psychologically from infant
to adult, and historically as we develop more and more
advanced civilizations.

Let us move beyond the threshold of consciousness to
the first level of consciousness, which we have labeled
collective consciousness. By collective consciousness we
mean that level of conscious awareness which is typical of
the mass mind. Such a mind has all its faculties and may
even be intelligent, but it does not see very much. Such
a mind simply "sees" what everybody else sees—trees, but
no beauty or botany; sky, but no poetry; and sounds, but
no sine waves or musical harmonies. The collective mind
thinks and acts as does the group; in fact, such corporate

identification is so great among certain primitive peoples that the anthropologist Levy-Bruhl describes this manner of living as "participation-mystique," meaning the feeling of oneness with whatever one perceives or thinks about. Such a failure to discriminate one's self and other persons or objects unfortunately describes the majority of so-called "modern" men just as accurately as it describes so-called "primitive" men. As a matter of fact, is it not the major concern of the average man to "fit in" unnoticed and "well adjusted" within the group? Is not the sheep-like trend toward conformity and anonymity all too evident in the contemporary over-abundance of collective man in the totalitarian state, and the other-directed man, the "organization man," and the "status-seeker" in today's democratic state? [13] Such primitive or under-developed awareness is unfortunately true of the uncreative majority of all civilizations, regardless of time or geography. Little can be done with such maximally encapsulated men; the most realistic answer is to provide such sheep with creative and imaginative leadership.

Specialized consciousness, the next level in Figure 14, represents the major target of this book. Why draw a bead on a quality of awareness which is obviously superior to the awareness level of mass man? Because the man of specialized consciousness is a man of considerable insight and importance, he is a man of special information, a man of learning, a man who changes the culture. He is, in short, one of Toynbee's "creative minority," and thereby a major agent of history.[14] Such men set the patterns by which the non-creative majority live; such men are thereby more dangerous than mass man. While it is important that all men become relatively unencapsulated, it is particularly important that the "creative minority" become unencapsulated. Toynbee's point regarding the importance of the creative minority is that these men represent the *source* of maximal creativity in our society and that such creativity must be nurtured with great care. Why? Because creativity is the source of values, and values must continually flow from a civilization if it is to continue to grow.

My point in relating the problem of encapsulation to the creative minority is that encapsulated or partial views of life are distorting; they lead to partial conceptions of truth and partial ways of living. The usage of the words "distorting" and "dangerous" are not accidental, for we have recently lived through a period which provides a case in point. The Nazi ideology is clearly an example of the kind of "dangerous" and "distorted" movement which can emerge from the encapsulated creative minority. (See pp. 23-25 for a related discussion on idolatrous misconcern as the distorted religious core of historical movements such as Naziism.) Nowhere is this more obvious than in the partial way of life of contemporary Western man. Western man has sold his soul for the rational-empirical, practical, scientific *Weltanschauung*. His accumulation of philosophic systems, scientific understanding, and practical gadgetry are impressive and provide great insights into the nature of outer reality. But Western man's inner nature, his intuitive and emotional aspect, has been neglected or even suppressed, so that his appreciation for the humanities, the arts, and religion are stunted, particularly when contrasted with his magnificent empirical-rational growth. Eastern man, on the other hand, represents an opposite situation. He has stressed the intuitive and emotional approaches to reality to the neglect of the scientific the technological, and the practical. This does not mean to imply that the Easterner does not have emotional or psychological problems. Such problems are universal. There is, for example, some evidence that the Eastern man is more "repressed" than his Western counterpart. Such repression manifests itself in a higher proportion of psychosomatic disorders in the East. I hope it is clear that my reference to intuitive and emotional in this context takes us back to the four approaches to reality as described in Chapter 2. Each of these specialized views of man and the universe is enlightening, but obviously incomplete and misleading. While oversimplified, such an analysis of the East and West carries enough truth to hurt, and certainly when the analysis is taken in terms of individual men in various parts of the world, it is unfortunately true that most of them are mass men and that those few who are more aware, those of the creative minority, are not fully aware, but at best only partially aware. This point has, in fact, been the major theme of this book.

How do we move on to greater awareness? At this juncture we approach the apex of awareness, the heights which few have scaled. For we now come to that rare phenomenon among men, the whole man, or what I have labeled individuated consciousness. (See Figure 14.) By individuated consciousness I mean that consciousness which sees maximally with all the psychobiological equipment at one's command. By individuated consciousness I mean that degree of awareness which is touched by perhaps too much reality, the ecstatically painful reality of the "outsider." [15] I mean the enlightenment of the East, known variously as *satori* (Zen), *samadhi* (Hindu), or *nirvana* (Yoga); or better yet, the kind of enlightenment which would emerge from a union of East and West.[16] In the terms of this essay, I mean the type of awareness which accompanies the unencapsulated, or multi-rail reality image. (See Chapter 2.) I mean the world-view which insists on a total psycho-epistemological foundation. As a specific example, I mean the total consciousness which characterizes Jung's individuated man. Since the term individuated consciousness leans heavily on Jungian thought, and since the road toward individuation or unencapsulation is central to the theme of this essay, it is important that we explore the concept of individuation further.

The process of individuation involves moving beyond the "participation mystique" of the mass man or the unconsciousness of the tribal group, which characterizes the infant, toward a highly differentiated and integrated ego. Such a self-realization process runs through a series of crises such as adolescence, falling in love, marriage, childbirth, middle age, and old age. The implication is that if the person is fortunate these crises will provide him with the opportunity to become more aware of who he is.

Let us take Jung's four functions as an example of how the individuation process unfolds developmentally. Jung says there are four major psychological functions—thinking, feeling, intuition, and sensation. Very briefly, the sensation process tells you something is there, the thinking process makes the discrimination as to what it is, the intuitive function tells you about its possibilities, and the feeling function reveals its subjective value. While it fails to capture subtleties and meaning due to its brevity, the essence of the four functions is caught in the following quote from Hall and Lindzey:

> Suppose that a person is standing on the rim of the Grand Canyon of the Colorado River. If the feeling function predominates he will experience a sense of awe, grandeur, and breathtaking beauty. If he is controlled by the sensation function he will see the Canyon merely as it is or as a photograph might represent it. If the thinking function controls his ego he will try to understand the Canyon in terms of geological principles and theory. Finally, if the intuitive function prevails the spectator will tend to see the Canyon as a mystery of nature possessing deep significance whose meaning is partially revealed or felt as a mystical experience.[17]

Jung's view is that the first half of life demands that the young person be primarily concerned with such extrovertive matters as getting an education, getting married, getting a job, and having children. Such outward-going concerns imply that the person's innate tendencies dominate the development of the personality. Thus, a person's naturally strong function will be primary during this phase of life. If one is to achieve wholeness it will be necessary to become more introverted during the second half of life, turning one's psychic energy inward so as to become more aware of the dark or undeveloped side of the psyche.

Since Jung's scheme is conceived in opposites, one must have an inferior function which is relatively undeveloped. Thus, we can picture a typical thinking-dominant type as shown in Figure 15. The lower half of the figure is shaded, indicating those psychic involvements which are relatively unconscious. The typically one-sided thinking type is characterized by a highly differentiated thinking function and a highly undifferentiated or unconscious feeling function. The other two functions are shown as partially conscious and partially unconscious. That secondary function which is relatively more differentiated is spoken of as the auxiliary function. Thus, theoretical scientists, such as Darwin or Einstein, would be examples of the thought-sensation type. Such thinkers must relate their theoretical schemes to the realities of the senses. The thinking-intuitive person, on the other hand, such as the speculative philosopher, is content to let inner revela-

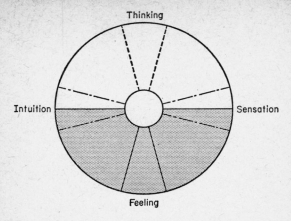

Fig. 15. The thinking type in Jung's analytic psychology[18]

tions or unconscious processes guide his thoughts. In both
of these thinking types, the thinking function is highly
developed, whereas the feeling function is relatively
primitive.

If a thinking type is on the road toward individuation,
his feeling function will become more active during the
second half of life. If the self of the first half of life
becomes too solidified, and if the psyche fails to respond
to crisis-clues, then the inferior function will remain
inferior, and the unconscious will ferment but remain un-
answered. Such psychological lopsidedness, by definition,
cannot help but lead to subsequent psychological difficulties. The person who responds to the unconscious, however, will move in the direction of self-integration or
wholeness. This implies an attuning to the messages of
unconscious processes and a recognition of the necessity
for developing one's undernourished functions. Thus, this
kind of development represents a greater differentiation
or involvement of each of the four functions. As this
development progresses, the individual moves toward a
greater and greater integration of these functions into a
unified self. It should be obvious that such a process is
never-ending. No living person can achieve perfection or

complete individuation, for as one function moves into greater awareness others are, of necessity, somewhat submerged. This tension of polarities continues for life, but presumably with greater and greater control and equanimity as the psyche approaches true psychological equilibrium due to the more equitable distribution of psychic energy.

This exposition is, of course, highly oversimplified for the purpose of conveying the basic idea of individuation. Little mention is made, for example, of the fact that each of the eight basic compound types is further complicated by the attitude of introversion or extroversion. Furthermore, nothing was said of Jung's concepts of persona, shadow, anima, and animus.[19] All of these enter into Jungian thought and therapy as the person struggles with his "self." If there is true individuation there is, of course, unencapsulation, for with individuation the person comes to terms with inner reality. In other words, he achieves greater self-awareness.

Are there levels of consciousness beyond individuated consciousness? This question is left open and unanswerable by pointing to an unknowable ultimate consciousness (see Figure 14) just as we postulated an unknowable ultimate unconsciousness. Presumably, ultimate consciousness is synonymous with God or ultimate reality, implying omniscience or complete awareness. If there are states of awareness which come closer to ultimate reality than what we have described as individuated consciousness, we in the West are not sufficiently cognizant of such states. It is, however, conceivable that the East has evolved techniques and insights which go beyond our Western methods. Just as the West has taken conceptions of outer reality (i.e., science) beyond Eastern conceptions, so it may be that the East has taken conceptions of inner reality beyond Western conceptions. Here is a vast area which is essentially untapped and is just beginning to be explored. It is to be hoped that the recent launching of a new oriental journal, *Psychologia*, will provide one of the necessary international bridges for greater understanding of such phenomena. My own impression is that Eastern awareness does *not* go beyond the level of individuated consciousness.

Eastern insights are, of course, shrouded in more mystery and mysticism than are those of the West, and they naturally move toward wholeness or enlightenment via a different path. The final goal, however, seems to be very much the same. Eastern methods are typically more introverted, intuitive, and esthetic. Japanese tea gardens and years of meditation are essentially alien to the Western mind. How many Americans would react favorably to 20 to 30 years of disciplined meditation as a member of a Zen monastery in pursuit of greater awareness? How many Westerners would be willing to submit completely to the zealous authority of a Zen master? And we simply take our sport activities differently, unhappily too often as spectators instead of with the complete awareness and immersion of the Zen archer or fencer. Perhaps the spectacle of the bullfight is Western man's most esthetic and "real" counterpart of Eastern sport-like activity. In general, however, the spiritual discipline and intuitive depth of the East unfortunately passes us by, thereby leaving us at a relatively unconscious level of self-awareness. I suspect, therefore, that it is simply the East's greater development of inner reality which makes it appear that it has developed levels of consciousness which go beyond the individuated level. Just as the West has gone overboard in the objective direction, the East is lopsided in the subjective direction. If we are, however, to use the analogy of exploring outer space, already on the planet Mars or Jupiter in terms of inner space, then we in the West had better keep our minds open for such insights, for the probabilities are high that the exploration of inner space is at least as important as the exploration of outer space.

EDUCATING THE GENERALIST

The various levels of consciousness which have been described and discussed suggest that the way we cultivate mind is the most important approach to the development of unencapsulated man. Different societies cultivate the minds of man in a wide variety of ways, but the formal or institutional way they go about this is via their schools and colleges. Perhaps we shall simply have to accept the fact that by the time each citizen comes to a university he has already been highly socialized, and thereby encapsulated, by the explicit and implicit norms of the culture, and that there is little we can do to change him. This may, in fact, be true, but we can at least raise the question of whether our formal, higher-educational system contributes to hardening the cover of the capsule surrounding the student or whether it is attempting to break the shell. I fear the answer is that the current situation in higher education is working hand in glove with the other cultural forces in the direction of encapsulation. I think the reason stems primarily from our over-concern with technical skills and "specialization" as opposed to liberal ideas and "generalization." The need for specialist education has been forced upon us, and we all understand and recognize this need as due primarily to the fantastic accumulation of knowledge during the past three or four centuries. The degree of detailed information which has piled up in each of the specialized areas of knowledge is staggering! The number of technical journals published today runs high into the thousands! There are, for example, over 500 journals which are closely enough related to psychology that they are searched continuously for inclusion in *Psychological Abstracts*, a journal which provides the only possible solution to keeping up with the psychological literature of the world. It briefly abstracts the leading publications on the subject. Similar journals exist in the other major disciplines of knowledge. Books are published so rapidly that expanding university libraries are ready for further expansion within a few months of the time they move into the added wings. Microfilming and reading-projector machines are now standard library equipment, a very handy procedure for conserving space while at the same time providing what would otherwise be rarely used and bulky but necessary source material.

Most doctoral candidates take around five to eight years to get their degrees rather than the three to five years which is the popular misconception. One reason they take so long is that they must pass examinations in two foreign languages, usually French and German. In many fields the foreign language requirement is a nonfunctional, archaic hurdle, a left-over from the middle ages when it would have been impossible to carry out scholarly work without facility in more than one's native tongue. But in the meantime the need for other skills, such as a knowledge of mathematics, anthropology, or neurology, may also be important. So the candidates may be required to learn these too. But such a candidate may find it difficult to learn those aspects of mathematics or neurology he needs without taking certain prerequisites. He may need elementary anatomy, physiology, physics, and chemistry, for example. In the meantime, back in his own department, the need for narrower and narrower specialization in terms of converging on a doctoral dissertation continues apace. While all this is going on, the professors in the land are busily engaged in proliferating courses for the already overfed cafeteria college catalogue. As the professor gets deeper and deeper into his particular specialty (e.g., Chaucer) within the area of his field (literature), he requires that more and more detailed seminars be offered on the subject. So that, whereas previously we might have had a course on 14th-century literature, we now have not only a course on Chaucer, but perhaps Chaucer I and Chaucer II. Thus, in spite of the obvious sarcasm and in defence of specialization, it seems fair to say that the overload of knowledge is now so great that specialists are needed in order to probe deeper into the mysteries of life. And, in fact, it would not be inaccurate to say that the demands for proficiency in the various compartments of knowledge are so great that they actually require all the energy a serious student can bring to his chosen specialty.

Granting the legitimacy of this view, we may now examine the impact of such narrow education on the personality of the scholar. I am granting that the specialist, as scholar, is needed, and that he makes important contributions to advancing the frontiers of knowledge. It does not follow, of course, that only the specialist contributes to knowledge, for it should be obvious that the broader perspectives of the generalist also provide new insights. The crux of the issue would seem to lie with our earlier discussion of inner and outer reality.

For we can easily see that the specialist may well provide us with a deeper awareness of a particular aspect of outer reality, but that such awareness, in and of itself, adds little or nothing to inner reality. Stated another way, to the extent that the super-specialist of today's world carries this way of doing things over into his personal life, he remains a specialist in the art of living as well as a specialist in making a living. This applies to the specialist scholar as well as the specialist in business or industry. For, in Jungian terms, such a person is not individuating; he remains with his dominant function and never brings his inferior function into consciousness. Such lack of self-awareness means, for example, that there is a very severe unconscious tension between the highly developed primary function and the underdeveloped inferior function. The difference in potential is very great indeed, and as long as such an enormous polarity continues, it will evoke a compensating response from the unconscious. Jung uses the analogy of a difference in electrical potential at this juncture, and implies that greater psychic energy flows in such a situation, just as it does in an electrical field. The implication of Jungian thought on this issue is that the above described sequence will occur even if the specialist is a great scientist or a great artist. No matter how meaningful the contribution to our understanding of outer reality, that person's inner reality will suffer to the extent that he ignores the totality of his psyche.

A similar concern for bringing about a coalescence of opposites lies at the core of Eastern thought; however, Easterners pursue the goal in a typically intuitive fashion. In this connection the Zen training technique known as the *koan* is of particular relevance. The *koan* is a specialized question-and-answer tactic which involves the presentation of a paradoxical question, expression, or action by the master for student meditation and response. *Koans* are of great variety in terms of paradox, ambiguity, and specific purpose. In toto, they are concerned with keeping the psyche open, not just the intellect, but more importantly, the senses, feelings, and intuitions as well. It is a technique designed to force the individual out of his well-worn ruts into new ways of seeing into a broader awareness. To manufacture a too simple example of the *koan* tactic, let us suppose that one of the students asks the master, "What is the Buddha nature?" The master might reply with some such remark as "Worm!," "You!," or he might simply point to a blade of grass or a mountain top. As the student progresses he may be presented with something essentially unanswerable, such as "What is the sound of one hand?" or "A girl is crossing the street. Is she the younger or the older sister?" One goal of such maneuvering is to coerce an experience of the limitations of the intellect and to force the individual into himself and his inner resources. A Westerner would say it represents a tapping of the unconscious. In other words, more emotional and irrational responses well up to the surface, and a greater feeling of vitality follows the deep frustration. The *koan* is particularly designed to bring out a naïve or phenomenological awareness, devoid of abstract names and labels; the stress is on the "eternal now" and the "suchness" of experience. "Such awareness is a lively attention to one's direct experience, to the world as immediately sensed, so as not to be misled by names and labels. *Samadhi* . . . is the perfection of the . . . pure experience, pure awareness, wherein there is no longer the dualism of the knower and the known." [20]

As the student develops, the *koans* become more difficult. The master may check a monk's awareness by some such question as "When the bath-water flows down the drain, does it turn clockwise or counter-clockwise?" Or he may require that a certain *koan* be responded to very indirectly, or without a verbal response. The adaptive but non-verbal response to a paradoxical situation is highly regarded. For example, the Zen literature[21] reports the story of how Po-chang, a Zen master, selected a new head master. He called all the monks together and set a pitcher before them, saying: "Without calling it a pitcher, tell me what it is." One of the monks said, "You couldn't call it a piece of wood." At this the monastery cook kicked the pitcher over and walked away. He was put in charge of the monastery. It should be pointed out that the first man's response was quite good, but it was only correct in the negative sense. The second

monk pointed directly to the essence of the matter by
his immediate, decisive, and insightful action. The spirit
of Zen is to point to reality, for students of Zen feel that
the real in any ultimate sense is ineffable and therefore
incapable of being taken in by words and concepts.

I see the *koans* as a graduated series of existential shock
treatments, miniatures of life's frustrations and ambiguities, placed in the path of the maturing monk as intuitive
practice in dealing with the demands of life. It is a tactic
for forcing the individual out of his skin. It is a way
of saying that life is, at best, paradoxical and that schemes,
systems, and philosophies are fine as far as they go,
but they cannot possibly be equated with life. Thus,
Zen itself must not be seen as a philosophy or religion,
but rather, as a way of liberation or unencapsulation.
More specifically in terms of the present context, perhaps the Western mind will see a way to borrow a page
from Eastern wisdom on how to educate away from
specialism and narrowness, particularly as it relates to
self-awareness.

Clearly, the problem of how to educate in the 20th
century calls for serious review—review of what the content should be, the manner in which such content should
be organized, and the tactics to be used in conveying it.
This is a situation for which the application of the principles of *gestalt* psychology would obviously be helpful;
for we need to refocus on the problem, that is, perceive
it in terms of the present highly congested state of
affairs, not in the simpler terms of 500, 100, or even 50
years ago. Some of our assumptions will need re-exam-
ining. Certainly the unchecked movement toward detail, over-specialization, and trivia must be stopped. The
argument here is not to eliminate specialists, but rather,
to move in the direction of producing educated specialists
rather than merely technical specialists, and to produce
generalists as well, that is, people who profess no particular specialty, but whose purpose in life will be regarded as legitimate and serious as opposed to that of
the dilettante. Unfortunately, the current scene, being
one which reflects an essentially encapsulated outlook,
is one in which only the specialist can speak or do
with authority and legitimacy. He who aspires to a truly

generalist orientation toward life, he who desires a liberal education in the tradition of the early liberal arts degree, will find few occupational niches for people so educated.

About five years ago American industry did a lot of talking about the need for liberally educated college graduates, sent out literature to this effect, and sent representatives to a variety of college-industry conferences presumably by way of promoting this concern. Those of us closely associated with American higher education noted, however, that when it came to the actual hiring it was the narrowly, but technically "tooled-up" specialist in economics or engineering who got the job. When the chips are down the attitude is that a broad education is nice, but irrelevant to getting the job done. What job? Turning out toilet seats, selling automobiles, or building rockets to send to the moon. The basic attitude toward the Renaissance man is that he belongs in the Renaissance, or at best, if he is wealthy it is all right for him to learn about such esoteric matters as Shakespeare, art, and architecture, and such useless things as history and philosophy, because it won't be necessary for him to earn a living anyhow. Contemporary education is evidently more concerned about earning a living than in living itself. Unfortunately, the educational curriculum at least partly reflects the values of society, and in much of the world today the vocationalism of higher education is forced upon it by the demands of society. Thus, on the North American continent, business and industry provide financial support to collegiate institutions primarily in terms of backing practical or applied fields of study. The so-called backward countries of the East and Africa, in need of scientific and production technicians, send their young people to this country for technical skills which they can use in the solutions of practical problems back home. There can, of course, be no objection to meeting these needs. The objection comes in promoting these practical, vocational needs to the exclusion of generalist needs.

Who needs generalists? Perhaps not Minnesota Mining and Machinery or General Motors, although a good case could be made that they, in fact, do need generalists.

For the point is that humanity needs generalists. Humanity needs generalists who are willing to make the attempt to understand the totality of things; humanity needs generalists who, by their outstanding ability to amalgamate and synthesize the contradictions and opposing polarities of living, symbolize the higher reaches of what it means to be; and finally, humanity needs generalists in positions of world leadership who will make decisions based on knowledge and wisdom. On this last point C. P. Snow[22] takes the position that humanity's need for generalists is so great that nothing less than the survival of human kind is at stake. The point is that the need for generalists is practical as well as theoretical. And while it would be too much to expect General Motors to take on generalists when they are needed primarily by humanity, if we could convince humanity, General Motors would eventually follow suit. Toynbee's writings suggest that the best place to start in giving humanity what it needs is with the creative minority—the artists, scientists, and the other creators of our civilization. And the best way to contact the creative minority is through our colleges and universities. In short, then, a practical beginning in answering the question of how to occupationally support the generalists is to provide jobs for them in our institutions of higher learning. Let us provide generalist education for generalists who will begin by teaching others to become generalists.

What would this generalist education be like, and what effect might it have? This idea is so new that it goes back hundreds of years to the original conception of a liberally educated man, and in the wake of industrialization, urbanization, organization men, and the specialization of society, we simply lost the ball. How might we retrieve it? My guess is that we can at least move in the right direction by turning away from narrow specialism and vocationalism toward a broad education and the liberal arts. Because of the very great forces of fragmentation in contemporary life we need to exert ourselves explicitly toward providing educational situations where integration, both outward and inward, can be maximally fostered. Exactly how this is to be accomplished remains to be seen, but the first step is to realize that this is a major problem for contemporary man.

While my experience with integrated-generalist education is necessarily limited and probably biased, I should like to reflect briefly on my five years of involvement with such efforts as one indication of the kind of vital experience which can emerge from this approach. As was mentioned in the preface, my exposure to this type of education is based primarily on several inter-subject seminars. The design of such a seminar involves experts from several pertinent disciplinary backgrounds focusing on a common problem. The exact nature of the topic is of no great consequence, although it should be broad enough to allow for multi-disciplinary consideration. The five seminars in which I participated involved one year (three hours of seminar per week) on each of the following: Science and Civilization, The Nature of Institutions, The Nature of Man, Standards of Judgement, and Philosophy and Psychology. Similar seminars have carried such titles as The Administrative Process, Society and Ideas in Flux, and First Principles. It is important that there be diversity in background among both professors and students.

For this particular type of seminar it is also extremely important that the student participant have a thorough background in at least one discipline. In other words, we are here discussing a case of generalist-specialist education, as opposed to purely specialist or purely generalist education. It is commonly referred to among the Ford Foundation project participants as "the room with a view" kind of education. One's specialty is one's room; the view is gained by exposure to the other disciplines represented in the seminar. Unless a student comes into such a seminar as a specialist, he cannot participate actively and thereby learn optimally. He must be well acquainted with a domain of knowledge so that he can dissect its structure and communicate this to others. We found in our undergraduate seminar on Science and Civilization that students without this kind of background were unable to get the feel of the seminar. They were confused, uncertain, and lost. In short, they did not have the necessary background and maturity to profit from such a high-level effort at synthesis. I might add that several of the undergraduates who participated were from the Able Student Program, a pool of students who are not bound by the usual course requirements, who are, in effect, put on their own. The point is that they represent people of outstanding ability, but that they simply lacked the necessary maturity level; they did not yet have a room from which to gain an integrated view. It is my impression that students below the level of senior could rarely profit from an educational experience of this kind, but that outstanding seniors who are potentially creative people could profit greatly.

Our procedure varied considerably, depending upon the participants and the particular seminar, but it essentially involved a formal presentation on the part of either a student or a professor, followed by discussion. It was my experience that the formal presentation was best if it was fairly short, say around 30 minutes, but meaty. It might even be appropriate to say that it was good if it was dogmatic. By this I mean that the leader who opened good discussions was the one who presented a clear and forceful point of view without too much hedging and over-qualifying. The corrections and qualifications usually emerged later in the discussion. Obviously the discussion was of the greatest importance. This was the real educational value of the seminar, for this is where the opposition and diversity of views came into contact with each other and were resolved. A problem would be kicked back and forth, turned upside down, and looked at from every conceivable relevant and sometimes irrelevant perspective. In the process specific knowledge from a variety of fields was learned, but, more important, over a period of time, one began to get the "feel" and the methodology for literature, government, history, or philosophy. After a while the participant gains real insight as to what they are "trying to get at" in literature, science, or art. And while nobody is expected to become particularly proficient outside of his area of special competence, what finally does emerge is a new awareness, a realization of the validity and power of great art and great science as legitimate approaches to knowledge.

One thing that happens frequently is the best evidence I know for the de-encapsulating effect of such an educational experience, and I suppose it happens most dramatically to the professors. An early professorial attitude goes as follows: "This will give me an opportunity to properly educate my colleagues about my field. This will give me a chance to get across to them how much we know and how my field contributes to the advancement of mankind." A later attitude is: "Today I will get an opportunity to learn more about X field of study. It's fantastic how limited we are in dealing with such and such a problem in my field. Perhaps I'll get an insight as to how they go about it in X field today." In short, the early attitude works, and the professor really does teach his colleagues something, but the undertone of arrogance and certainty gives way to the later attitude. The new insights gained into how alien ways of knowledge go about their business provide such new vistas that very frequently the original room is considerably redecorated. The overwhelming impact of new ways to see, thought based on different assumptions, methodologies foreign to one's nature but relevant to another domain of knowledge, is so great that one almost bursts from the deeper and broader sense of reality.

The step toward unencapsulation is, of course, a very real shock; it is quite comparable to the loss one suffers when a loved one dies, or if one is shedding a religious framework. But this is true education! This is learning where it hurts! When education reaches you where you live, it is real, it is powerful, it is existentially valid. This is the kind of education I experienced as a participant in the above mentioned multi-disciplinary seminars. I can assure you that this involvement represents some of the highest moments of my life, and I have deep-seated doubts as to my willingness to return to the usual way of educating.

This is just one program, aimed primarily at the graduate student, and primarily concerned with synthesis. But it opens up a broad avenue of similar possibilities, and it may serve to open our minds to equally valid generalist approaches. My most recent venture along these lines involved offering a seminar with a sociologist-anthropologist on The Nature of Man. We dropped certain courses listed independently under sociology and psychology and offered one common course instead. Similar collaboration could be done in joint courses in personnel management on the part of economists, psychologists, and sociologists. It would eliminate duplication and make the course more exciting by having three professors in the classroom at the same time. Pomona College is experimenting with a senior divisional inter-disciplinary course under a grant from the Carnegie Foundation. If the student is majoring in art or music, for example, he takes a one year inter-disciplinary seminar in Fine Arts; if he is a history major, he takes an inter-disciplinary seminar in Social Science; if a physics major, he takes it in Natural Science; and so on.

Efforts at generalist education are not new, and there are many good things to be said in favor of the kind of general education courses which were initiated two decades ago at Columbia and Chicago. What makes the above-mentioned courses different from previous efforts is the stress they place on simultaneous multi-disciplinary presentation. To put it another way, professors cannot provide integrated education for students by way of a curriculum or a set of survey lectures. Each student must do the job of integration for himself. But, professors can provide an optimal setting within which the integration is to occur, and it appears that the inter-disciplinary seminar is one such setting.

The answer to the objection that this is expensive education must be in the affirmative—it is. But so is all really good education, and, in my opinion, it would be silly not to figure out ways to get around the expense. We manage when the problem relates to the production of "hardware" such as bombs, rockets, and Sputniks. I assume that if we are willing we can also do it when it comes to "headware."

THE UNENCAPSULATED REALITY IMAGE

We have assumed that it is desirable to move in the direction of unencapsulation as opposed to encapsulation, and further, that there may be ways of optimally educating in terms of such a goal. Assuming further that such education can actually have the desired effect, what might this unencapsulated man look like? Would he in fact, be desirable, or like so many illusory goals, turn out to be some kind of a monster? There is, of course, no way of really knowing until we try him out, but I am obviously willing to take a chance on him. Let us make some guesses as to what he might look like in contrast to the encapsulated man, keeping in mind that the dichotomous contrast is only by way of exposition of something we know to be a matter of degree.

To begin with, he would be liberally educated as opposed to narrowly educated, generalist-integrated educated as opposed to specialist-fragmentary educated. If he were a specialist, he would be a generalist-specialist rather than a specialist-specialist. Presumably this broad outlook would minimize the probability of provincialism on social and political issues. We should expect him, therefore, to be relatively free of the currently prevalent petty prejudices of race, color, religion, political party, and country. We would see him, then, as essentially a free citizen of the world or the universe, with his loyalties moving down from the highest unity of universal, planetary, or world government, to national, state, or local government. His depth of understanding and breadth of vision would certainly not allow him to stumble over the petty business of depriving others of freedom also, even though they may look different, talk differently, dress differently, or come from afar. Presumably he would be able to live out the idea of unity within diversity.

But let us focus on the broadest possible consideration of the question of the nature of the unencapsulated man by looking at his reality image, for it is his reality image, and how he projects it and lives by it, which is the crucial item. We have said, in effect, that the unencapsulated man is one who projects the broadest and deepest possible reality image, whether he projects it outwardly in terms of comprehending the universe, or whether he projects it inwardly in an effort to comprehend man.

What is the nature of the unencapsulated man's reality image when he projects it on to outer or objective reality? In the terms of Chapter 2 of this book (see especially

Figure 1) he would approach reality via all four epistemological routes. He would not generate an encapsulated world-view based only on science or only on religion. Furthermore, in order to meet the requirement of depth, in addition to that of breadth, he would be much concerned about epistemological criteria and the emergence of new approaches to knowledge. This would mean, for example, that he would not be taken in by reductionistic approaches to knowledge such as logical positivism, nor would he fall into the trap of confusing a subjective experience with objective reality, as in the case of "revealed" truth.

The unencapsulated man would be particularly interested in what F. S. C. Northrop has called epistemic correlations.[23] An epistemic correlation is simply an agreement reached through two or more valid approaches to reality. This concept can best be explained by reference to Figure 1. (See page 12.) Note the several dotted lines labeled with capital letters. Line A, for example, connects the rational and intuitive approaches to reality, whereas line B connects the empirical and rational approaches. Line C represents a linkage of three approaches, and line D connotes an agreement among all four approaches. The implication is that if a finding is reached via two or more criteria of "truth" that its probability of "really" being true is enhanced. Thus, linkage A represents a convergence of a particular item of the rational and intuitive epistemological approaches. A major reason for the relative epistemological stability of scientific findings is due to its insistence that both the rational and empirical approaches mesh. Unless a finding is eventually confirmed as a true epistemic correlation in terms of the rational and the empirical, it simply has no status within the scientific enterprise. The implication of epistemic linkages C and D is that further confirmation in terms of the remaining approaches to reality would render the finding even more probable.

If we now broaden this way of looking at epistemic correlations to include the interpenetrations of reality images, we see that the broadest possible image of reality is the one most likely to provide us with true vision. In fact, if there could be such a thing as a convergence of all legitimate reality images, the implication of letter E is that we would have transcended the epistemological barrier and come to know ultimate reality. Such metaphysical transcendence is impossible, of course, for the type of awareness which would be required in this case represents the epitome of awareness, namely, the requirement that one be omniscient and, in effect, *be* ultimate reality. While this is impossible for finite man, it is possible for him to break the bonds of psycho-epistemological encapsulation and emerge with the broadest possible reality image, as represented by line D. In other words, while he cannot attain ultimate consciousness, he can reach for it. In short, he can at least move on beyond specialized consciousness to individuated consciousness. (See Figure 15.)

Let us now project unencapsulated man's reality image inwardly. What do we have? Again, we have the same man projecting a reality image in terms of all four ways of knowing (see Figure 1)—that is, in terms of thinking, feeling, sensing, and believing. The only significant sense in which we are restricted in our approach to truth relates to limitations in taking in insights which come to us via all four approaches. And what is perhaps more important, to the extent that we minimize any one or more of these natural psychological processes we reduce the fullness of being. The person who approaches reality by only one epistemological route, for instance, is bound to have a myopic view. While it does not follow that the person who approaches reality with all his faculties will necessarily penetrate the reality barrier any better than the monorail reality seeker, it does mean that his multi-approach will give multi-rewards in terms of living out man's full potential, and further, that his multi-image is at least less likely to be distorted. Because of his great efforts at synthesis we would expect such a man to be highly self-actualized, that is, integrated in the Jungian sense of a life-time struggle toward wholeness or in the Eastern sense of reaching for *satori*. Again, it would mean reaching beyond lopsided or specialized self-awareness to individuated consciousness. (See Figure 14.)

There is a metaphysical speculation to the effect that

the microcosm is a miniature or a mirror image of the macrocosm. The implication is that man, as microcosm, is a reflection of the macrocosmic universe. Knowledge of the one presumably leads to knowledge of the other. Our analysis of unencapsulated images of inner and outer reality suggest that this microcosm-macrocosm polarity is either an identity or represents complementary aspects of an emergent unity. Perhaps this type of insight is what allows the enlightened Easterner to "go with" the universe and the individuated Westerner to be at peace with himself. The harmony which results from the union of opposites, whether in terms of man and the universe, microcosm-macrocosm, approaches to reality, Jungian types, male and female, or East and West, is a major theme of this book. For the implication is that such merging of opposites represents a creative union, thereby releasing the single greatest potential for individual and social growth—creative expression. Further, the nature of this growth is clearly toward wholeness, thereby being by definition a growth of the spirit. It is in the name of such spiritual growth, which means progress both for the individual and civilization, that I offer this plea for the release of contemporary man from his state of encapsulation.

To be more specific, the implication here is that creativity will occur at its highest levels if the creative minority is relatively highly individuated, rather than highly specialized as they are in contemporary life. The rare insights which would emanate from such minds would be bound to convey a luminous quality because of the total meanings which they would necessarily reflect. Here we are touching on the qualities of greatness in men. The Schweitzers, Einsteins, and Da Vincis, no matter what specialized field they start from, are never contained within the confining capsules of convention, time, or place. Such unencapsulated men see and live widely and deeply, and stand as models for lesser men, more encapsulated, to follow. For reality-as-a-whole demands a total approach; it demands the type of openness that only the totally functioning or unencapsulated man can provide.

As I see it, such a man, the man who is engaged in a lifetime quest away from encapsulation, moving in the direction of the broadest and deepest possible reality image, has the key to what it means to be and to see. He is thereby representative of man in his deepest and most significant sense. For such an orientation would mean that he was very much alive in the best meaning of the term "existential" and very much aware in the best meaning of the term "philosophical." Such a man would be a man of great compassion, great sensitivity, and great thought. He would, in short, be reaching for ultimate consciousness. And while it is true that such an open approach to life is very risky for the individual man in the short view, it is clearly more creative and productive, and therefore, more viable for all men in the long run.[24]

NOTES

1. This is, in fact, the view taken by Aldous Huxley in *The Doors of Perception*, New York: Harper & Bros., 1954. The same theme is developed by Colin Wilson in *The Outsider, op. cit.* The probabilities are high that it was in this sense that outsiders Van Gogh and Nietzsche went "over the deep end."

2. For some introductory insights along these lines see the very readable *The World of Mathematics* (four volumes), edited by James Newman, New York: Simon and Schuster, 1937, and E. Courant and H. Robbins, *What is Mathematics?* New York: Oxford University Press, 1941.

3. M. Wertheimer, *Productive Thinking*, New York: Harper & Bros., 1945.

4. See, for example, L. L. Thurstone, *Primary Mental Abilities*, Chicago: University of Chicago Press, 1938; J. P. Guilford, The Structure of Intellect, *Psychological Bulletin*, 1956, 53, 267, 293, and J. W. French, *The Description of Aptitude and Achievement Tests in Terms of Rotated Factors*, Chicago: University of Chicago Press, 1951.

5. Stephen Polyak, *The Retina*, Chicago: University of Chicago Press, 1941.

6. See the writings of Donald Griffin. For example, Navigation of Birds, *Scientific American*, 1950, 182, 52-55.

7. This is our conception of consciousness. For a more thorough discussion of consciousness see pp. 171-183.

8. H. B. English and A. C. English, *A Comprehensive Dictionary of Psychological and Psychoanalytic Terms*, New York: Longmans, Green & Co., 1958.

9. Reference to unconscious processes as "the unconscious" requires explanation. Although the noun form is the most widely used, it is incorrect and misleading because it leads to reification, or the ascribing of thinghood or empirical reality to concepts whether they actually qualify for thinghood or not. Referring to a degree of awareness as "the unconscious" implies the same kind of empirical reality as when one says *the* rock or *the* book. There is no part of the brain which can properly be referred to as "the unconscious," as such reification suggests. In short, it should be understood that the term "the unconscious" is merely a conventional and largely misleading usage for a state of awareness.

10. See the papers by J. G. Miller, Discrimination without awareness, *Amer. J. Psychol.*, 1939, 52, 562-578, and (with A. Sterling) Conditioning under anesthesia, *Amer. J. Psychol.*, 1941, 54, 92-101.

11. H. B. English and A. English, *op. cit.*, pp. 111-113.

12. E. G. Boring, *The Physical Dimensions of Consciousness*, New York: The Century Co, 1933, p. 234.

13. See Aldous Huxley, *op. cit.*; George Orwell, *op. cit.*; Erich Fromm, *op. cit.*; David Riesman, *op. cit.*; W. H. Whyte, *The Organization Man*, New York: Simon and Schuster, 1956; Vance Packard, *The Status Seekers*, New York, David McKay, 1959; and Milton Mayer, *Madison Avenue*, New York: Harper & Brothers, 1958. You may wish to refer back to Chapter 5 at this juncture.

14. See Arnold Toynbee, *A Study of History* (two-volume abridgement), Cambridge: Oxford University Press, 1946-1947.

15. See Colin Wilson, *The Outsider*, *op. cit.*

16. See F. S. C. Northrop, *The Meeting of East and West*, *op. cit.*

17. C. S. Hall and G. Lindzey, *Theories of Personality*, New York: John Wiley, 1957, p. 87.

18. J. Jacobi, *op. cit.*, p. 13.

19. For a short but sophisticated treatment of Jung's concepts see C. S. Hall and G. Lindzey, *op. cit.*, pp. 76-113. For an extensive treatment of types see C. G. Jung, *Psychological Types*, New York: Harcourt, Brace & Co., 1923.

20. Alan Watts, *The Way of Zen*, New York: Pantheon Books, 1957, p. 52.

21. For a brief summary, see *Ibid.*, p. 129.

22. See C. P. Snow, *The Two Cultures and the Scientific Revolution*, New York: Cambridge University Press, 1959, and

Science and Government, Cambridge: Harvard University Press, 1961.

23. F. S. C. Northrop, *The Logic of the Sciences and the Humanities*, New York: Macmillan, 1947.

24. Although some eight years have transpired since the writer actively initiated this volume, I still find it extremely difficult to bring closure to this effort because there is so much of importance which has not been adequately covered. But this inadequacy is clearly in the nature of the task, particularly when one attempts to encompass so large a domain. But, the essential impossibility of the task remains even if we descend to the more mundane level of trying to keep up with new books which have come out during the time of writing. The logical conclusion of attempting to achieve such a goal is an infinite regress, for it really would not be possible to achieve closure if one insisted upon including all, or even most, of the recent relevant statements in print. Here, then, are five such books which were not included, but would have been had the author had the time.

T. J. J. Altizer (editor), *Truth, Myth and Symbol*, Englewood Cliffs: Prentice-Hall, 1962.

E. T. Gendlin, *Experiencing and the Creation of Meaning*, Glencoe: The Free Press, 1962.

O. H. Mowrer, *Learning Theory and the Symbolic Process*, New York: John Wiley, 1960.

M. Polanyi, *Personal Knowledge*, Chicago: University of Chicago Press, 1958.

P. Wheelwright, *Metaphor and Reality*, Bloomington: Indiana University Press, 1962.

Index